Mary Virginia
~ April 1981.

FAITH
for the
JOURNEY

Bruce Larson

FAITH
for the
JOURNEY

Fleming H. Revell Company
Old Tappan, New Jersey

Scripture quotations identified KJV are from the King James Version of the Bible.

Scripture quotations identified RSV are from the Revised Standard Version of the Bible, copyrighted 1946, 1952, 1971, by the Division of Christian Education of the National Council of the Churches of Christ in the United States of America, and are used by permission. All rights reserved.

"The courage that my mother had" by Edna St. Vincent Millay is from COLLECTED POEMS, Harper & Row. Copyright © 1954 by Norma Millay (Ellis).

Portions of this work appeared previously in the author's book *Believe and Belong*.

Library of Congress Cataloging-in-Publication Data

Larson, Bruce.
    Faith for the journey.

    1. Christian life—Presbyterian authors.   I. Title.
BV4501.2.L323   1986   248.4′851   86-10113
ISBN 0-8007-1491-1

Copyright © 1982, 1986 by Bruce Larson
Published by the Fleming H. Revell Company
Old Tappan, New Jersey 07675
Printed in the United States of America

Contents

	Introduction	9
1	Hitting the Road	15
2	How the Journey Begins	21
3	Where Will You Be When You Get Where You're Going?	29
4	A New Passport	37
5	The Road to Gethsemane	47
6	How to Love Your Traveling Companions	57
7	The Road to Cana	65
8	The Road to Your Place	73
9	The Roads Where Jesus Walked	81
10	Handling the Roadblocks	91
11	The Road to Bethany	99
12	Detours on the Road of Faith	107
13	The Road Home	117
14	The Road to the Stable	125
15	The Last Road	133
16	The Road to the Empty Tomb	143

Introduction

LIFE IS A journey. It begins with birth and ends with death. In between the two we travel on many roads and take some nasty detours. But, make no mistake about it, life is movement forward. To stand still or to turn back is death, no matter how we disguise it.

For the Christian, the journey is even longer. It begins not with conception, but in the mind of God, and continues after death into eternity. We are pilgrims moving toward the City of God, restless, never at home in this world; yet, paradoxically, laying down our very lives to improve the lot of our brothers and sisters in this world, simply because we are under orders so to do by the Lord Himself.

It is tragic that so many of us think of true spirituality as the contemplative life—a life of meditation, prayer, and withdrawal from the world. If this were true, then our patron saint should be someone like the great Buddha we see in those familiar statues, inert, passive, with lids closed over inward-looking eyes.

But this is not the picture that the Bible provides of those first faithful pilgrims. What do we read in that holy chronicle? We find the story of Adam and Eve leaving Eden in exile; Cain becoming a wandering fugitive; Noah building an ark for an incredible journey; Abraham and Sarah equating the will of God with giving up home and friends and all that is safe and familiar to become wandering nomads for the rest of their lives. It is the story of Joseph being sold into slavery by his brothers and living among foreigners all his remaining years; Moses and the Israelites wandering on the Sinai Peninsula for forty years; a new generation of Israelites moving forward across the Jordan to claim the land of promise and being told by God that they will receive only that portion which they, by walking on it, claim in faith.

It is the story of Jesus, the Messiah, calling the twelve and training them by walking with them over the rough and dusty roads of Palestine for three years; the early church sending their finest out to the ends of the earth to share the good news and to establish churches.

It is impossible to read the Bible and not see the importance of roads: the roads of Galilee, the road to Jericho, the road to Bethlehem, the Emmaus Road, the Gaza Strip, the road to Egypt, the path through the Red Sea, the ford of the Jordan, the road to Damascus, the roads of Asia Minor, and the road to Rome.

In two thousand years of church history, the luminous saints who have become our role models are, for the most part, those whose home is the highway and whose faith is in the Christ who travels the road with them. We honor those legions of wild-eyed fanatics in the tradition of the Apostle Paul who have crossed oceans in small boats, scaled snowy mountain passes in sandals, or braved death at the hands of hostile tribes in steamy, mosquito-infested jungles to carry the good news and physical aid to remote peoples.

Martin Luther walked all over Germany and from there to Rome and back. John Knox spent his early Christian years as a galley slave on an enemy ship. John Wesley traveled hundreds of thousands of miles on horseback all over

England, preaching on the average of four times a day for fifty years. And in our own time, who does not admire Pope John Paul II for his peripatetic zeal in being a missionary to the uttermost parts of the earth? Truly ours is a traveling faith. After Jesus says, "Come unto me . . ." He commands us to "go. . . ."

The Christian faith is for people on the move, people pursuing the vision of a new heaven and a new earth. Authentic faith is to start the journey, one on which we are fed, sustained, and encouraged by God and His people. The temptation for each of us, according to the biblical record, is to yearn for the fleshpots of Egypt once we have begun our journey in the wilderness, to have set our hand to the plow and then look back.

This book looks at some of the roads most of us will take in our lifetime. It suggests that when the road becomes difficult or unbearable or we become confused or lost, we can put our faith in a Person who has promised never to leave us nor forsake us. Though the road may be fog enshrouded, we are never alone. With the Lord as our traveling companion, the journey is bearable and the destination certain.

FAITH
for the
JOURNEY

CHAPTER ONE

———

Hitting the Road

I WONDER IF you can truthfully say that you enjoy a long trip with your family in the family car. Someone has said, "Traveling with children is always traveling third class." I think most of us have mixed feelings about traveling with the family.

Let me tell you about a family trip we took about fifteen years ago when our three kids were small. It was to be the trip of a lifetime—a six-week-long journey from New Jersey all through the South, down into Mexico, back up the West Coast as far as Seattle, and then home across the continent by the northern route. We started out in July in a nonair-conditioned Volkswagen bus. We were five in all, plus one neurotic dog, a springer spaniel with very long hair, which was shedding and blowing around that car for six whole weeks. Actually Duke, the dog, had a nervous breakdown on the trip and never fully recovered. He was partly cata-tonic the rest of his life. We had bought a tent especially for this trip—a great, big pyramidal tent—and out of deference to my wife and daughter we got one with a bottom in it in the event of bugs or snakes. On the first night of camping out, somewhere in the Carolinas, our dog relieved himself in the tent. It was never the same again.

I can remember the scenes of endless fighting. The three

15

kids in the backseat argued constantly about who did what and why. I'd like to forget the many times I drove at sixty miles an hour with my left hand on the wheel, my eyes straight ahead on the road, and my right hand reaching back, swinging furiously, trying to punch somebody, anybody, yelling, "Stop it. Quit it. Don't do that anymore!" I particularly remember the afternoon we reached the Grand Canyon. We had saved for years for this trip, and there we were coming to one of the all-time biggies of the sightseeing world. "Children, look," I cried, "there is the Grand Canyon." They'd look up from their Walt Disney comic books and say, "Very nice," and go back to Uncle Scrooge and Donald Duck. I'd say, "Listen, you're here to look at the Grand Canyon. You could have read those comic books at home."

One special memory is of running out of gas in Mexico out in the middle of nowhere. We just sat for hours until finally an old peasant came along and siphoned some gas out of his battered truck into our car. He wouldn't even take any money. He just said, "No, glad to help." I remember driving across the Mojave Desert on a two-lane, no-passing highway behind a truck full of dead cows on their way to a rendering plant. We spent two hours behind that truck in 120-degree temperatures, going about thirty-five miles an hour. Then there was the night when, arriving in Portland to visit friends, I asked the kids to get the dog and put him in the backyard. There was no dog. We had left him at a gas station 100 miles back.

These are some of my memories of our once-in-a-lifetime trip. But believe it or not, when our family gets together now as five adults, that trip is one of the great events in our memory bank. We reminisce at length and always end up saying, "Wasn't that a great trip!" And somehow it's true. Why is that? I think it's partly because a trip like that is a unique means of discovering something about ourselves and about each other. Traveling with somebody else reveals a lot about the person we are—our resources, our disposition, our habits. We learn good things and bad things. It's a short course in self-awareness. We learn things about the people with us, good and bad, and usually we end up feeling closer to each other. In spite of the catastrophes, accidents, and difficult times, somehow the five Larsons and that poor dog came closer together. And I think most of all we discovered that God was adequate for our mistakes, our shortcomings, our bad tempers. God was there in tangible ways blessing us.

I believe God has a journey in mind for all of us. I'm convinced that whenever God wants to do something new or teach us something, He takes us on a trip. There is no better way to reveal Himself to His faithful people than to get them on the road traveling with Him. That's what He did with the Israelites when He brought them out of Egypt. For forty years God traveled with His faithful people. They left Egypt and wandered in the Sinai Peninsula, which is something like the Mojave Desert, where there was almost no water and no vegetation.

A friend of mine in Chicago, Dr. Robert Charnin, did his dissertation on the logistics of that trip. He came up with certain statistics by using the Book of Numbers plus present day computations. He has estimated that 3,600,000 people left Egypt. Seventy Israelites went there originally, and if they stayed 420 years and doubled their number every 25 years, that would be the size of the group making the Exodus. If every family had an average of 2 sheep, 1 cow, 1 camel, and 1 donkey, that would add up to 5 animals per family, or about 3,600,000 animals. He tells us that if those people plus animals marched 50 abreast there would be a line 123 miles long.

Dr. Charnin has also estimated the supplies needed for that group. Let's say that in the desert you would use 1 gallon of water per person per day and 2 gallons per animal. It would require 1,080 railroad tank cars of water a day to keep them going. Then there's the manna. There was no food and God supplied anew each day some kind of frosty, protein substance that forms on the rocks. The animals and the people survived on that for 40 years—no Big Macs, no Kentucky Fried Chicken. The actual meaning of the word *manna* is "What is it?" They were hungry and when God sent them manna that first morning, the people said, "What is it?" And they ate "What is it?" for 40 years. No home-cooked meals, no peanut butter. The manna required to feed the animals and the people would fill 160 boxcars a day.

In those 40 years the Israelites must have learned a lot about themselves and about God. In the midst of 40 years of births and deaths, God was sending 160 boxcars of manna and 1,080 tank cars of water into the desert daily. Most present-day Jewish theology comes out of the recorded history of what God did on that incredible journey and it's no wonder. Bear in mind that all of us who are Christians are Jews as well. The Exodus is an important part of our history.

God revealed Himself to the people in this journey for forty years until a whole new generation was ready to inhabit the Promised Land. But after they had left Egypt and gone through the Red Sea (and, by the way, marching fifty abreast at two and a half miles an hour, it would take forty-nine hours to cross), God spoke these words as they began this journey: "Now therefore, if you will obey my voice and keep my covenant, you shall be my own possession among all peoples; for all the earth is mine, and you shall be to me a kingdom of priests and a holy nation" (Exodus 19:5, 6 RSV). God was saying that it might take a journey of forty years for them to discover that the earth is His, that they belonged to Him, that they are a family, a nation of priests and blessers. Within those forty years He revealed Himself as someone able to take care of all their needs. The Exodus is one of the great trips in all history because God revealed to us who we are and who He is.

God has always had His people on a journey. Abraham wandered most of his life from Ur down to the Palestinian area. Jesus, when He began His ministry, took twelve people on a three-year journey. He must have considered that the fastest way for them to discover who they were personally, who they were as a family, who Jesus was, and who God is. Saint Paul was an itinerant missionary, always on a journey. In *Pilgrim's Progress* John Bunyan paints life as a pilgrimage, suggesting that we Christians are on the way, moving from here to someplace else. All of this seems to point out that a journey is the best means of revealing who we are, our strengths and weaknesses, our faith or lack of it.

We Christians are all on a journey. The Bible reminds us that we are traveling toward that city not built with hands but eternal and made by God. The city in which we live can be some kind of pale foreshadowing of that Eternal City, and those cities that we dwell in for a time ought to be different because we are traveling to the City Eternal in the Heavens. And so faith is motion forward. Faith is not just simply what you say or what you believe. Thomas Carlyle said years ago, "If you do not wish a man to do a thing you had better get him to talk about it. For the more men talk the more likely they are to do nothing else." That's why we need to do more than to sit around and preach and talk and think and study about the faith. Faith requires that we move out for forty years or three years or even three weeks. We are in motion because God is out in front calling us to be in motion. Identity comes from direction. We learn who we are as we begin to move forward.

Katherine Anne Porter writes in her book *Ship of Fools,* "I'm appalled at the aimlessness of most people's lives today; fifty per cent don't pay any attention to where they are going; forty per cent are undecided and will go in any direction; only ten per cent know what they want, and even all of them don't go toward it." Terrible things happen to people, she says, like those in *Ship of Fools,* and they don't learn by it. They go into their graves the same shapeless creatures they were in the cradle.

God says to us as He did to the people of the Exodus, "Get up and get moving. I will go with you. You will be a Nation of Priests. You will learn who you are and you will learn who I am." For years I had a sign in my office that said, "Life is not a problem to be solved, but an adventure to be lived." And that's what God is saying to us. Let's focus on the adventure before us as we move toward that invisible and eternal city.

CHAPTER TWO

How the Journey Begins

A FRIEND OF MINE is a professor at an Ivy League school. He told me about a conversation he overheard at a cocktail party he went to some time ago. The head of the astronomy department was speaking to the dean of the divinity school. The astronomy professor said, "Now, let's face it. In religion, what it all boils down to very simply is that you should love your neighbor as you love yourself. It's the Golden Rule, right?" "Yes, I suppose that's true," replied the dean of the divinity school. "Just as in astronomy it all boils down to one thing—'Twinkle, twinkle, little star.'" I think we all have a tendency to want to make truth so simple that it's ridiculous. We can then say, "Well, if that's what it is, forget it."

Nevertheless, I would suggest to you that the essence of life consists largely of one simple truth: the art of knowing when to say yes and when to say no. These are the words that determine the direction and quality of our lives. You say yes or no to continuing your education. You say yes or no to a particular job. You say yes or no to a possible promotion that might change your whole life. You say yes when you join a church and become a part of a specific community of faith. You say yes or no to a marriage prospect. Perhaps you've been regretting some of the no's you said before you eventually said yes. I heard about a wealthy bachelor who died and left all of his money to three women to whom, he said, he owed all his earthly happiness. It seemed all three had said no to his proposals of marriage.

If you're a parent you find yourself saying yes or no at all sorts of crucial times in the lives of your children. In the famous biblical story of the Prodigal Son and his father, think of the courage of the father. When the son asked for his inheritance in order to leave home and go out and explore life, the father said yes. That was surely one of the high-risk adventures of all time. For parents especially, so much seems to hang on when to say no and when to say yes. Even presidents have this problem. William Howard Taft's young son was once overheard being rude to his father. "Are you going to rebuke him?" someone asked. "Well, I thought about it," was the reply. "Now, if he was speaking to me as his father, he deserves a serious rebuke, but if he was speaking to me as President, then he stands on his constitutional rights."

When to say yes and when to say no. All of life depends on these decisions. If we can't say a clear yes or a clear no, we are in trouble. We're like the man whose psychiatrist asked him after many sessions, "Don't you think you have a problem with decision making?" "Well, yes and no," was the answer. When we say both yes and no, we are in big trouble. I'm told that industry tries to hire executives who can make decisions clearly and quickly. "Yes, we'll build this; no, we'll scrap that program." If they're right 50 percent of the time, that is good enough. They're looking for people who have the courage to say yes or no. They don't always have to be right.

But the faith journey also begins with a yes-or-no decision. In the biblical understanding, *faith* is a verb, not a noun. Faith is something we do. It is not something we have.

We can't go out and get faith. Most of us already have a bucketful of faith. We live by faith. We have faith that other cars will stay on their own side of the road. We have faith that the water in our tap is not poisoned. Faith is something we already have. The point is what are we doing with it? I believe this is the biblical understanding of faith. Faith is not saying, "True," to a concept. When God spoke to Abraham, He asked him to do something—to leave the familiar and go into a new land. He asked Abraham to begin a pilgrimage that would take an undetermined number of years. Abraham replied by acting. He did not say, "Oh, I see. What an amazing concept. The theology of discipleship, I must write about that sometime." He had the choice of saying yes or no to God. He said yes and he went.

Moses, as well, was not asked to say, "True," to a concept but yes to a plan of action. When God met Moses at the Burning Bush, He asked him to do something. "Will you go down to Egypt and lead my people out? I want them liberated." Moses could have said, "Ah, the theology of liberation. What a revolutionary concept. I've never read anything on that subject." At first he said no, which is legitimate. But ultimately he said yes and he went.

And then there is the incredible story of Mary, that brave girl who met an angel at the well in Nazareth. The angel might have said, "Mary, good news and bad news. The good news is that the Messiah is coming. The bad news is that God thought He ought to be born of a virgin, and you've been chosen if you will say yes." Mary was not asked to accept the theology of incarnation. She had a choice of saying yes or no. She said yes; she was willing to enter into this experiment with God.

Jesus met some fishermen by the sea and asked them, "Will you follow me?" What might they have said? "Well, you see, we've got some theological problems. We heard some strange rumors about your birth. We really can't buy that story that your mother was a virgin." But Jesus was not asking them to accept difficult concepts. His question was simply, "Will you follow me?" He would deal later with their theological problems. Just then they did not need to understand all things—who He was, how He got there. A simple, clear yes was all that was required. I think there is a key here to finding spiritual wisdom. So often we preachers have tried to teach doctrine assuming that when you understood enough doctrine, you would say yes. I think we have it backward. When you say yes, spiritual wisdom follows by some mysterious work of the Holy Spirit.

In our understanding of God, you and I have a choice. Is God a concept or is He a person? If God the Creator, the inventor of you and me, is a person, then you cannot respond by saying, "I believe." Suppose someone has said to you, "I love you. You are the most wonderful person I've ever met. I want to live my life with you. Will you marry me?" You can't answer by saying, "True." That's not relevant. If someone says, "I love you. I have offered to give you my life, will you give me your life?" You can't respond with a, "True," or, "False." If we're talking about theological concepts or mathematical equations or philosophy or forms of government, we have true-or-false options. We can say, "I believe," or, "I don't believe." But the very word *believe* in the Greek means "to commit to something." For the Christian, to believe is to fling your life after a person.

A man came to see me recently about some problems. In the course of our conversation I asked him, "Are you a Christian?" "Well," he said, "gosh, I sure try to be. I've had some great days and some bad days. I've been very faithful to God at times in my life. Right now I'm not sure." I said,

"Are you married?" "Oh, yes," he said. "How can you be so sure you're married? Are you a great husband?" I asked. "Are you always there when needed, always generous, always kind, sensitive, loving—all these things—in your marriage?" "Oh," he said. "No." "But how do you know you're married?" He said, "Well, because I stood up and said before witnesses, 'Yes, I take this woman.' " I said, "You can do that with Jesus, and you can do it right now if you want to." He wanted to and he did. And I've had a number of people in my office in the short time I've been back in the pastorate who have been believers all their lives but who had accepted Christian concepts and beliefs rather than saying yes to a person.

That was true of me. I grew up attending a Presbyterian church, one of the great churches of Chicago. I can't remember a time that I did not believe that Jesus was the Son of God, the Savior who died for the sins of the world and my sins. But my life was changed in Stuttgart, Germany, during World War II, when I kneeled all by myself in a bombed-out building and said, "Jesus, if You really are the person I've always believed in, I give You my life right now. I cannot promise that I will be good or faithful. I want to be. I don't want to be who I am, but I can't promise that I will change. I hope that You will change me."

Faith is a matter of choice. In the Old Testamant, we read that Joshua gave the people this choice: "I have given you a land for which ye did not labour. . . . choose you this day whom ye will serve . . ." (Joshua 24:13, 15 KJV). That same choice is ours today. Most of us worship in churches we didn't build; we live in a land that has come to us through faithful people of past generations. But our choice now is whom we will serve. We can serve the gods of money, wealth, power, or religion, or we can serve the Living God.

This is the choice that Jesus gives you right now. The challenge is not complicated. It is a simple thing to say yes in a marriage ceremony. You stand up before witnesses and commit yourself to someone else for the rest of your life. But the consequences are enormous. Saying yes to a marriage partner or to God means a lifetime of faithfulness, which isn't easy. But the initial yes is very simple. You never have to wonder if you're married or if you're a Christian. You can say no, or you can say nothing—which is no. The real test is who is running your life? It's not whether or not you have good days or bad days, days of good faith or days of doubt and despair. On the best days or the worst days, who do you say is in charge of your life?

Over the years I have counseled any number of people who were wrestling with this yes-or-no decision. When I worked in New York, I would often suggest they walk with me from my office down to the RCA Building on Fifth Avenue. In the entrance of that building is a gigantic statue of Atlas, a beautifully proportioned man who, with all his muscles straining, is holding the world upon his shoulders. There he is, the most powerfully built man in the world, and he can barely stand up under this burden. "Now that's one way to live," I would point out to my companion, "trying to carry the world on your shoulders. But now come across the street with me." On the other side of Fifth Avenue is Saint Patrick's Cathedral, and there behind the high altar is a little shrine of the boy Jesus, perhaps eight or nine years old, and with no effort He is holding the world in one hand. My point was illustrated graphically. We have a choice. We can carry the world on our shoulders or we can say, "I give up, Lord, here's my life. I give You my world, the whole world."

Perhaps you have loved Jesus all your life, but have you said yes? You're probably going to have theological problems the rest of your life. I hope you're smart enough to have theological problems. That means you're thinking about faith. In Jesus Christ, God says to us, "I have bet Myself on you, each one of you. I'm committed to you. I belong to you now. Will you follow Me? Will you say yes?" When you do, your journey of faith begins.

CHAPTER THREE

Where Will You Be When You Get Where You're Going?

A MINISTER FRIEND in New England sent me a sermon he preached recently on the topic "Where will you be when you get where you're going?" And, of course, the whole mystery of your identity that we probed in the last chapter is tied up with where you're going.

Most of us tend to describe ourselves by telling what we do for a living. But you are not your job. Your job is not your vocation. Suppose you were living 2,000 years ago and had an opportunity to ask the Apostle Paul, "Who are you?" One possible answer could be, "I'm a tentmaker. I am a very efficient, competent, creative tentmaker. My bids are competitive. I have up-to-date designs. I think I am one of the best in the business. I spend forty or fifty hours a week making tents. On the side, I do a little preaching and some small-group work." This might be a largely accurate answer. The majority of Paul's time was spent making tents—at one time with Priscilla and Aquila. Forty or fifty hours a week might have been occupied that way. But somehow I don't think that would be his answer to your question. I think he might say something like this, "I've been called by God to bring the Good News of Jesus Christ to the world. Incidentally, I make tents and I spend a good part of my day doing that."

Ananias, the man who was sent to pray with Paul in Damascus, was an ordinary layman with a steady job. Perhaps he worked in the local sandal factory. He might have been a moneylender. He might even have worked in some first-century fast-food chain. The point is he had a job and he was supposed to go to work on the morning the Lord spoke to him about visiting Saul. He was told something like this, "Don't go to work this morning. I've got a job for you. Phone in and say you'll be late." He argues at first. He's sure the Lord has made a mistake. But finally he obeys. Ananias knows his vocation is to serve the Lord. His job is simply a way to make his living.

I love the Old Testament story of the Prophet Amos. He is no professional holy man. He arrives in the Washington, D.C., of his time with a message for the king, "We are in big trouble as a nation." They ask who he is, very likely in tones that convey, "Who do you think you are, anyway?" He replies, "I am not a professional prophet. I am not a seminary-trained preacher. I am not a philosopher. I'm a shepherd and a fig-picker. That's what I do for a living fifty, sixty, or eighty hours a week. But my vocation is to come here and warn you that we are in serious trouble and to suggest what we should do about it."

Your vocation and your job are not necessarily the same. You may work forty hours a week to make a living, to pay the rent, and buy the groceries. While your real vocation takes only five hours a week. That may be the time when you teach a class or do volunteer work at the hospital or whatever. In those five hours you're busy with the work you're called by God to do. If that's the case, you're in the company of Amos, of Paul, of Ananias, and a great host of biblical people who had both a job and a vocation.

Then there are those people for whom the job and the vocation are parallel. That's a special privilege it seems to me—to have a job in the area of your vocation. But it is also easier to confuse the two. And they are not quite the same. For example, teaching is a job not a vocation. Your vocation is to call forth gifts in students and motivate them to learn. Practicing law is a job; your vocation is to see that there is equal justice under the law individually and corporately. Medicine, whether you're a doctor or a nurse, is a job, but healing is a vocation.

For you mothers or fathers who stay home and care for your families, homemaking is simply a job, but nurturing people is your vocation. We're told that John Wesley's mother, Susanna, had eleven children and yet she spent an hour alone with each one every week talking to them about their spiritual life. She understood that running a household was a job but she had a broader vocation—to mold and shape her children. When I tell my wife that story, she always reminds me that Susanna had live-in help. Nevertheless, she took her true vocation seriously in the midst of her job. Mother Teresa reminds us that being a nun is a job but bringing the love of Christ to the hungry and dying in a teeming city is a vocation. Selling is a job; helping people acquire what they need, *really need,* is a vocation. Designing or constructing buildings is a job, but providing a better environment is a vocation.

Counseling is a job. Being a friend to those who come for advice is a vocation. Politics is a job; building a just and humane society is a vocation. Would that we had more politicians with a genuine sense of vocation. Preaching is a job—my job just now—but my vocation is to enable the people of God to be everything they are meant to be.

What are you hoping to accomplish with your life? When you get where you're going, where will you be? If you spend forty years being a lawyer, engineer, salesperson, nurse, what will you have accomplished? If God has given you a vocation along with that job, you will have accomplished a great deal. It's the old case of the means versus the end. Your job will not necessarily be your vocation. It may be simply a platform from which you can exercise your skills in pursuit of your vocation.

I heard about a businessman who turned his successful business over to his son and installed him as the new president. The company made drills of all sizes and shapes. Of course, the incumbent vice-presidents were very unhappy that they were to be working for this inexperienced young man. The first staff meeting at which the young man presided focused on long-range planning. The other executives were not exactly cooperative. The vice-president in charge of long-range planning said, "Pardon me, sonny . . . er, sir, but we have covered all this before. We know exactly what the market needs and wants. We are planning on everything from quarter-inch to one-inch drills, self-contained power units, hookup units, you name it, we have planned for it." The young man was patient. "This meeting is not to talk about drills," he explained. "There is no market for drills. The market is for holes. People are buying holes. They want triangular-shaped holes or square holes or round holes. Drills are simply a means to getting the kind of holes they want. Have you surveyed how we can make better holes by means of a drill, or anything else?" This young man did not confuse the ends with the means.

Jesus said, "I came that you might have life and have it more abundantly" (*see* John 10:10). Each of us separately has a calling from Him. There is something He has for us to

do and that calling is our vocation from which we never re-
tire. Jobs may come and go. I've known some exciting people over the years who have had this keen sense of vocation.
One of them was Ralston Young, a neighbor out in New
Jersey for many years. He was once written up in *Reader's
Digest* as "The Most Unforgettable Character I Have Ever
Met." He was the famous Redcap 42, and his job was to
carry bags at Grand Central Station in New York. His vocation was loving the people whose bags he carried. He said,
"Everybody taking a train out of Grand Central isn't going
on a honeymoon. Many are going to funerals. Many are
about to be separated from family and friends for a long
time. Some are going to prison." He held a prayer meeting
three days a week at twelve noon in a cold, unlighted railroad coach on track 13. All sorts of people usually turned
up—businessmen, secretaries, discouraged preachers. While
carrying bags, Ralston exercised his vocation.

Dr. Elisabeth Kübler-Ross has found her vocation and it
goes beyond medicine. She helps the dying and those who
care for them to understand the dynamics of death. Maggie
Kuhn, founder of the Gray Panthers, has found her vocation. She's encouraging senior citizens to discover that the
best years are ahead. Bill Stringfellow, a lawyer, described
by Karl Barth a decade ago as the greatest theologian in
America, became a Christian when he was studying at Harvard. He graduated from Harvard Law School at the top of
his class. Over lunch one day in New York he told me that
his vocation was not law. That was simply a job. His vocation was to see that the poor had access to legal representa-
tion. Stringfellow went to New York City's Harlem, rented a
cold-water, fifth-floor flat and opened his law practice. His
vocation was to serve the oppressed, the lowest and the least
of the land.

My mother, who died at ninety-three, had a vocation. Until she was eighty-five she was healthy and strong and full of vim and vigor. She worked five days a week full-time doing all sorts of volunteer work. She was an aide at Cook County Hospital. She sold secondhand goods in a thrift shop in the slums, and tutored a ghetto child with reading problems. When she moved to a retirement village, she lost her vocation and with it something of who she was and she began to fail appreciably, mentally and physically.

If you're trying to find your vocation, let me give you some guidelines:

1. *First of all, listen to God.* Let Him tell you what He is hoping you will be when you get where you are going. I believe God wants you to be accountable for a chunk of society somewhere, however small, and for their physical, mental, emotional, economic, or spiritual well-being. Be praying about that. God can make your vocation clear, as He did with Amos and the Apostle Paul.

2. *Claim your uniqueness*—no one has been where you've been. All the hurt, the pain, the gifts, and experiences that you have had have equipped you to see life as nobody else sees it. I know a woman who is writing books right now featuring handicapped children as the heroes and heroines— something that as far as I know has not been done as yet. She has a handicapped daughter and is writing out of some of the pain and the hurt and hardship of her own experience. Each of us has had life experiences unlike anyone else's. God gives us unique eyes to see the world around us and make our particular contribution.

3. *Be open to change.* Don't believe that you must be what you have been. William James, pioneer psychologist, wrote years ago, "The ideas gained by men before they are twenty-five are practically the only ideas they shall have in

their lives." If true, that's a tragedy. Be open to change and to growth in terms of your vocation. God may show you a whole new thing.

4. *Don't limit your possibilities.* Don't be discouraged by the fact that you are not a professional, that you don't have credentials. All of society seems to be breaking loose in this area. Someone wrote recently, "Our society is becoming accustomed to the 28-year-old mayor, the 50-year-old retiree, the 65-year-old father of a preschool child and the 70-year-old college student." We need to stop thinking we're too old . . . or too young . . . or not qualified.

5. *Simplify your life in order to pursue your vocation.* This may be the most difficult part. Pope John XXIII once said very wisely, "See everything, overlook most things, try and change a few things." Genius is to see it all, and then zero in on the one thing you want to do. The ability to simplify is the genius of good corporate management or the management of your life and mine.

Evolution is invariably from the complex to the simple. Aircraft engineers began by making a very complicated piston engine for planes. That evolved to a project with fewer parts, then to a jet engine with even fewer parts and finally to the rocket with the fewest parts of all. If you have a genuine vocation—a calling—you need to simplify your life to accommodate that calling. For example, a homemaker who wants to become a concert pianist better clean the house less and practice more. I suggest a little planned neglect in terms of the everyday job. You may not be able to pursue your vocation in addition to what you're doing now. Something may have to go. Make a decision to do those other things less often, that you may do more of the thing God has given you to do.

Sometimes I wish that by some miracle each of us would

have the interest on $2 million for the rest of our lives. We'd
be in the position of never having to make a living again.
We could not hide behind the fact that we are trapped in
some meaningless job. We would be forced to find out what
we really want to do with our lives. We would be free to discover from God our true calling.

CHAPTER FOUR

A New Passport

SOME JOURNEYS require a passport. We have to prove that we are who we say we are. Our passport photo is usually a poor clue to that. I've yet to hear anyone say, "Gee, I don't really look that good." There must be a better way to package our identity. Some people are using the want ads in an attempt to do that.

On a recent visit to Seattle our oldest son, Peter, who is a newspaper reporter, brought me the current copy of a large "underground" newspaper. He called my attention to the section called, "Personals." I want to share some of those "personals" with you. I do so without making any moral judgments, though that would not be difficult.

> Unhappily married fun-loving professional man in 40's sks. single woman for fun, dining and romancing.

> Single white male seeks close relationship but not marriage with tall attractive wf, vegetarian preferred.

> Single white male 5'5" looking for small woman. Interests are music, movies, golf and backgammon. Send picture.

> Soon to be paroled male looking for serious single female to correspond with. In 20's and aiming for self-improvement.

College professor and Marxist sympathizer looking for female who wants to help change the world. Must love cats.

White female who is tired of dieting is looking for male in mid 40s interested in a growth opportunity. Interests TV and eating.

Sophisticated 33-year-old male, educated in Europe, seeks gorgeous brown-eyed blonde with a great shape for disco and other fun and games. Send photo.

Serious-minded male in 50's wants to meet like-minded female—no smoking, drugs, or divorce. Must like classical music and museums.

Honest Christian Gentleman mid 50's seeking serious, faithful lady in her 40's for marriage. If honest and faithful, please reply.

When my son Peter read these to me he said, "Do you know, Dad, we could simplify all this if we had a Dewey decimal system for rating people. It would save so much time to say a 348.36 wants to meet a 517.93."

Well, I think Peter fully understood the frightening implications of these "personals." Whatever their intentions, honorable or otherwise, these people are trying to meet a member of the opposite sex by putting themselves on the market as a commodity looking for another commodity. They are presenting themselves as a package made up of age, sex, habits, and interests. They have lost their sense of personhood.

There is a battle going on between God and the enemy for our very souls. The classical writers of the past understood this clearly. In *Faust* we find a man who bargains with the devil. The devil wants to possess his soul, and he makes the offer attractive enough to close the deal. And exactly what is your soul? Your soul is who you are, your very essence, your identity, that which God had in mind before you were born. If you give that up, you have lost everything. We read in the New Testament, "What shall it profit a man, if he shall gain the whole world, and lose his own soul?" (Mark 8:36 KJV).

I am convinced that this ancient battle between God and our ultimate enemy still continues with us today. We may laugh at the devil, but his strategy is more powerful than ever. Albert Camus, one of our great existential writers and novelists, said, "Man is the only creature who refuses to be what he is." Zebras and monkeys, polar bears and butterflies have no identity problems. Only we humans have the capacity to deny who we are or to try to be something else.

I have a good friend who is a psychiatrist in the Black Forest area of Germany. Walther Lechler is a Christian and, I think, one of the most exciting and eclectic psychiatrists in all Europe. His clinic at Bad Herenalb is for alcoholics and general neurotics, people not unlike you and me. The brochure describing his clinic says, among other things, "Come here to discover that you are not the dwarf of your fears nor the giant of your dreams. Come and find out who you really are." You see, that is the most primal and basic search you and I are engaged in.

The personals in the underground paper point up the fact that there is a powerful force at work in our culture to rob us of our identity. This cultural force says that you are not a person, but a commodity. You are a thing. You are a package. You are a number. Look in your wallet and see how you are identified by the government or by your bank. You have a social security number and credit card. You are a number to the phone company and a five-digit zip code to your postman.

A few years back a popular movie suggested that we rate members of the opposite sex by numbers on a scale of one to ten. This is merely an extension of the idea communicated in the newspaper "personals." A newly divorced friend was telling me recently how totally unfulfilling the marriage had been. I asked, "Just why did you marry this girl?" "Because she was a fifteen!" was his answer. When we categorize other human beings as a three, a seven, a ten, or a fifteen, we are reducing them to commodities.

For centuries Christians have been trying to understand the term "the mark of the beast" in the Bible. Certainly one explanation is that there is an evil force who wants to replace your identity with a number. One of the central themes of the Bible is that when we encounter God, we discover that He wants to give us a name—our true name.

One of the Bible's many examples of this kind of encounter is the account of Jacob wrestling with an angel by the brook Jabbok. The first time I saw this lonely valley between low hills where a little brook still meanders, I was deeply moved. In my mind's eye I could imagine the struggle that took place three thousand years ago when that irascible son of Isaac and Rebekah was facing the crisis of his life. His past had caught up with him. He had cheated his brother, deceived his father, and tricked his father-in-law. The consequences were now crashing down upon him, and it was the dark night of the soul for Jacob as he wrestled with God all night by this hauntingly lonely and lovely brook. His opponent had crippled him, but Jacob persevered. Just before dawn he said, "I will not let you go unless you bless me." At that point, the angel said to him, "Who are you?" And the answer was, "Jacob."

Now Jacob is the name that his parents gave him. Remember that he and his brother, Esau, were twins. He was the second to come out of the womb and was born trying to grab his brother's heel. In Jewish custom the firstborn gets everything and the second, nothing. This little infant arrived in this world struggling to supplant his brother. A power struggle began very early on, as it does in your family and mine. And those witnessing that unusual birth said, "Look at little Cheat (or supplanter, for that's what Jacob means)." In all the ensuing years that was his name—little Cheat. But little Cheat became big Cheat. His family named him something destructive because they thought it was cute, and it shaped Jacob's life.

What name has your family given you? Who are you in their eyes? Do they say, "Here comes that mess; here comes the clumsy one"? "Here comes our problem child"? "Here comes the rebel"? Or do they say, "Here comes our darling—the precious one who can do no wrong"? Somewhere along the line the family name sticks, and you become that person your parents perceived you to be.

I heard about a minister's son who spent the whole night carousing and arrived home at 5 A.M smelling of strong drink. His father's greeting the next morning at breakfast was, "Good morning, Son of Satan." "Good morning, Father," was the cheerful answer. Unfortunately, most of us don't have the capacity to slough off the names our parents have given us as easily as that young man. Most of us tend to become what we are called.

Or, perhaps, even though your parents haven't given you a name with a negative connotation, they have nevertheless communicated somehow that you are of less worth than you really are. Brooks Adams, son of Charles Francis Adams, one of our former ambassadors to Great Britain, tells a moving story about his boyhood. Once his father took him fishing for a whole day. Brooks recorded that day in his diary, "Spent the day fishing with my father; it was the most glorious day of my life." He had had his father's attention for a whole day. And ever after, he kept referring back to that day as one that had changed his life. Years later, upon his father's death, he found among his possessions a diary for that same period. He looked up the entry for that memorable day and found: "Spent the day fishing with my son; a wasted day." His father may have loved his young son dearly, but, nevertheless, a day spent with him was a wasted day. If you are unimportant to your parents, they have given you a negative identity.

Even Jesus was labeled. We read in our New Testament about Philip's attempt to convince his friend Nathanael that he had found the Messiah. When Nathanael learns that it is Jesus of Nazareth, he says, "A Nazarene? Can any good thing come out of Nazareth?" (*see* John 1:45, 46). Nathanael was prone to label others by their regional roots. Society still does that. Oh, you're from Texas, or Hollywood, or Brooklyn, or Pumpkin Gulch. Right away we have projected an image of what you're like. You're already in a box because you are from the Bronx, Boston, or Peoria.

I think it's all part of the devil's plot to take away our individuality. In some societies (and ours is one of them) the term "senior citizen" has a negative label. The older person is no longer expected to make a contribution. But in a different society, older people are honored and respected and listened to. We are labeled by all sorts of things—our income level, our job, the clubs we belong to, even the church we attend.

What happens if you choose a college that stresses competitive sports? If you are an intellectual instead of a jock, you tend to see yourself as second class for the rest of your life. An athlete at a school that values academic achievement only has the same experience. Our environment is a contributing factor in terms of our feelings of worth.

In this whole matter of identity I believe that God wants to give us three great gifts. First He wants us to know *whose* we are. We belong to Him. The precise words in the Bible are, "Ye have not chosen me, but I have chosen you" (John

15:16 KJV). When we acknowledge that and say yes to God, we know whose we are. The most important decision any of us can ever make is to say yes to God's great affirmation of us.

But after we have settled whose we are, God can give us the gift of knowing who we are. When Jacob wrestled with the angel, he was actually wrestling with God, who was asking, "Who are you?" When Jacob answered, "I'm a cheat," God gave him a new name, erasing the name his parents had given him. His new name is Israel, which means prince. And from that moment on the cheat became a prince, from whom all believers since have been named. We Christians are the new Israel, named for the patriarch Jacob, whose name was changed.

Jesus gave Nathanael a new identity, as well—the same Nathanael who was so ready to label others by their hometown. We don't know what Nathanael's parents had in mind when they named him, or what meaning that name took on in the family structure. "Stupid Nathanael, lazy Nathanael, or bright and industrious Nathanael." But when Jesus Christ meets him He says, "Look here. This is a rare specimen. An Israelite in whom there is no guile" (*see* John 1:47–49). There aren't many of those around even now, Israelites or Presbyterians. Most of us have lots of guile. Jesus saw a man who was transparent, with no hidden motives. Nathanael must have been struck with the accuracy of this description, for he exclaimed. "How did you know me?" Jesus said, "I know you. I saw you under a fig tree before Philip called you." Nathanael's response is a declaration of faith, "You are the Son of God." God can do that for you and me as well. People around us—parents, spouse, friends—may never discern who we really are; but God can and does.

It's so liberating to realize we are special. I was reading

recently about Harvard University observing its 300th anniversary. In the midst of this great celebration, the freshman class came marching down the street carrying a banner that said, "Harvard has been waiting 300 years for us." Instead of worrying about their worthiness to be at a school with such an awesome tradition, they believed their presence would bring about Harvard's finest hour.

That's the kind of hope God gave Jacob when He named him Prince. Jesus gave a new name to Simon as well. He believed in him, believed that he would no longer be the impetuous, vacillating person he had been. He named him Peter, the Rock. Peter became a rock, the head of the church at Jerusalem. Jesus communicated to the least important woman in a Samaritan village that she was important simply by spending time with her and listening to her. He honored her questions and He asked about the most intimate details of her life. After that encounter, she ran through the town crying, "Listen! I have met the Messiah, someone who knows all about me and made me feel worthwhile. Whatever you all think of me, I've met the one who knows who I really am" (*see* John 4:1–42).

But after we find out whose we are and who we are, we discover that we are not alone. God gives us a new family. It is one of His choosing, not ours. All of us who are a part of a community of Believers did not choose the other members. We are God's gift to each other. He tells us whose we are, who we are, and where we belong. We belong to each other. We are blessers one of another—giving each other new names, calling forth hidden gifts, and being ministers one to another.

I met a minister like that when I was in the infantry during World War II. He was our battalion surgeon and his name was Doc O'Rourke. Doc O'Rourke had worked his way through medical school by playing professional football. He was a great, friendly Irishman with a big smile and flashing eyes. He was with us in the front lines of combat, the first to respond, along with the chaplain, to the cries of the wounded. The two men, carrying Red Cross flags and a litter, risked their lives countless times to rescue and care for the wounded.

Just once during combat I went on sick call to an aid station about two miles back from the front. It was just a basement with three walls. Most of the building had been blown away.

It was wintertime in the Vosges Mountains, bitter cold and snowing. It seemed as though there were a hundred of us lined up on sick call to see the harried battalion surgeon. Each man was asked first of all to open his shirt for an examination with a stethoscope. But each time before putting that cold metal on someone's chest, Doc would walk over and dip it into a pot of hot water. I was deeply touched watching that simple act. To Doc O'Rourke we were human beings. We were not just pieces of meat being patched up. To Doc O'Rourke each one of us was special. You and I have that same power to communicate to others that they are special. At home, in our schools, at work, we can let people know that they are important to God and therefore they are important to us.

The word of the Lord came to Jeremiah, the prophet, and he wrote these words, "Before I formed you in the womb I knew you, and before you were born I consecrated you; I appointed you a prophet to the nations" (Jeremiah 1:5 RSV). That doesn't apply just to Jeremiah. God thought of you before you were born and before your parents were born, and He called you by name. He had an identity for you. He still does. Don't settle for anything less. He'll issue you a new passport. You might even like the photo.

CHAPTER FIVE

The Road to Gethsemane

I HEARD OF A mother who returned home to find her two older sons sitting on top of their little brother, who was howling loudly. Asked to explain, they said, "Well, you see, he fell in the wading pool and we are trying to give him mouth-to-mouth resuscitation. The trouble is he keeps getting up and walking away."

The story reminded me again of how often the church has tried to minister the unnecessary to the unwilling. We try to make people religious, and I believe that's the furthest thing from God's mind. If we believe in a God who can meet all of our needs, then the Church of Jesus Christ ought to be the most relevant institution in all of society. He is the ultimate relevant being, and that's the point we need to get across to those who don't know Him yet.

If the church is to be relevant, we must talk to people about their deepest problems. In a 1978 poll 52,000 Americans were asked to name their most deadly fear. Way out in front was the fear of loneliness. Most of those who responded were trying to deal with or overcome loneliness.

Dr. James Lynch of Johns Hopkins Hospital has come up with the statistics to show that loneliness is the number-one physical killer in our time. He is an exacting medical researcher whose charts and graphs indicate that discernibly lonely people are most prone to illness and death.

Thomas Wolfe, the great novelist of forty years ago, said at the end of his life, "The whole conviction of my life now rests upon the belief that loneliness, far from being a rare and curious phenomenon, is the central and inevitable fact of human existence." So the evidence piles up from novelists, medical researchers, and public opinion polls that our number-one problem is loneliness.

If that's true, then we must all be experts in loneliness. Each of us could write a Ph.D. dissertation on the shape of loneliness in our own life. If we were asked, "What is loneliness?" we could compile a long list of answers from our own experience. Let's bear in mind that loneliness is not the same as aloneness. We can be alone and yet feel surrounded and supported by the people we have chosen to make a part of our life—sometimes even those who are no longer living. Or, we can be in the middle of a great crowd and be very lonely. Loneliness means being separated and cut off. It means being insular, having ingrown eyeballs to the point where we have no conscious connection with anybody else.

What do I know about loneliness? I recently compiled a list of what it means to be lonely, drawing from the events of my own life and the lives of my family or very intimate friends. Here are some of my personal descriptions of loneliness.

Loneliness is being single and aching physically and emotionally to share your life and your love with somebody else.

Loneliness is being married to the person of your choice, with whom you are still in love, and looking over at that spouse asleep in bed beside you and realizing that there are still large chunks of your life where loneliness reigns.

Loneliness is saying, "I love you," too late. The person who should have heard it is now dead, and all you can do is try to reach out to that departed soul and say, "I hope you knew, because I never could tell you before how much you meant to me."

Loneliness is having hurt your best friend, with no way to make it right.

Loneliness is starting an organization, inviting in your best friends, and having them vote you out.

Loneliness is being told that you have a serious illness and being unable to talk about it with anyone.

Loneliness is coming to the end of your life, having used up most of the options that God has given you, and being unhappy about what you did with them. You've traded your options for a whole lot of things that turned out to be worthless. It's like winning a supermarket sweepstakes—you run through the store and end up with a basket heaped full of frankfurters and beans.

Loneliness is being in the middle of a warm, friendly church and feeling that there is nobody there who really knows who you are.

Loneliness is having had religious parents who could only criticize, who could never affirm or hug or tell you you were neat.

Loneliness is being a sincere believer for a long time and coming to a place where you wonder . . . *Have I blown it? Did I take a wrong turn back there somewhere? Am I really in the will of God?*

Loneliness is being a coward in a crisis—when your vote or voice could have changed the decision of a committee or a group. The hour has passed, the moment is lost. You didn't speak and you're stuck with your cowardice.

Loneliness is having a secret sin so bad that you think nobody would like you if they knew.

Loneliness is not living up to other people's expectations (whatever that means).

All of us can make up a list of the times that we have experienced loneliness and allowed ourselves to be cut off from humanity, even from God, or so we think. I happen to believe in the devil, an evil force, the father of lies. He's a very close companion and I speak about him often. I believe that somehow he takes this inevitable fact of human existence—our loneliness—and turns it into a destructive force. Our culture is often the devil's best servant, and our culture has given us false expectations about life and what it ought to be. Our culture suggests there are four very basic ways of dealing with our loneliness.

First of all, we teach our children at a very young age that marriage is the answer to loneliness. Early on we hear as a child, and perhaps pass on to our own children, the story of the lonely girl with a mean stepmother and two ugly stepsisters. She has the blues and with good reason. Her clothes are grungy; she never goes to parties. When the rest of the family is out dancing, she's home cleaning the house. Poor old Cinderella is lonely, lonely. But one day a guy pulls up in a white Camaro with a glass shoe that just happens to fit her. They get married and what happens? They live happily ever after. So every child gets the message. Things may be tough just now but someday they'll meet Mr. or Miss Right. They will marry and they will no longer have the "lonelies." When marriage doesn't meet these expectations, most of us feel cheated. "Good grief!" we say. "I must have picked a lemon in God's grab bag of life. It's not supposed to be like this."

But of course it is. God loves us so much that He has put a longing inside of us for ultimate love, and no human relationship or circumstance will satisfy that. So the best and most fulfilling marriage, as good as it is, does not solve our basic loneliness. But we have given young people expectations of some problem-free state, and when that is not their experience, anger and frustration grow. All those happily married couples, especially the ones you meet in church, seem to have it made. They are always smiling. After the Couples' Club Potluck, we walk to the parking lot thinking, "How come I got stuck with him (or her)?"

Or, we are told that sex is the answer to our loneliness. That's what I resent most about so many of these slickly done contemporary magazines. We hear a lot of clucking about the nudity they feature, but that's not the most destructive aspect of these magazines. They are aiming at the lonely guy or gal out there and they are saying, "Hey, are you lonely? You don't have to be. Listen, if you have enough sex with enough people you won't have that problem." It is one of the biggest lies ever perpetrated on young people. The loneliest people in the world are hanging out in singles' bars and other similar places where casual sex is the deal. The Playboy philosophy, which promises intimacy and belonging, produces the very opposite. It produces alienation and self-hate.

Our culture also seems to promise that success is an answer to our loneliness: Be a success and you'll never be lonely again. If we can just get to the top in our profession—our business—we will be at the hub of a busy life, with people standing in line to be our friends. Yet you and I know that some of those people who have finally become chairman of the board are the most lonely of all—terrified at being at the top of the pyramid, of having someone discover how little they know. I think people at the top are even lonelier than the rest of us. Because they hold such power over the lives of others, they never can be sure that they are loved and appreciated for themselves. Famous rock stars seem to be tragic examples of the fact that loneliness grows in direct proportion to success.

Then there are those who believe the church is the answer

to our loneliness: If you become a Christian, if you really accept Jesus, if you are really filled with the Spirit, you'll never be lonely again. Unfortunately, that isn't true either. Certainly the church is in the business of offering intimacy and community, but that doesn't mean we will have all our problems solved. In every denomination just now, clergy divorces are more and more common. We are pressed to explain this in the light of the victorious life some have been promising believers. And the guilt laid on those who continue to have problems, especially in marriage, is enormous.

There is a story about an old Scandinavian couple, Sven and Hulda, who were both born-again Pentecostal Christians. He taught Sunday school, and she sang in the choir. They had a family altar and family prayers. They went to church twice on Sundays and attended the mid-week service. But they couldn't get along. They fought all the time. They felt very guilty about their stormy relationship and they prayed about it often. One morning after their quiet time of listening to God and praying, Hulda said, "Sven, I think I've got the answer to this hopeless problem we have. I think we should pray for the Lord to take one of us to be home with Him . . . Then I can go and live with my sister."

But even those who have fulfilling marriages and who are a part of a church full of genuine caring and community are going to experience loneliness some of the time. And I think that's part of God's plan. I really believe that loneliness is a gift of God. It is not something to be ashamed of or avoided. It's one of the best gifts God has given us. You and I were meant for belonging, intimacy, and community. We are to be an essential part of the Body of Christ, without whom the rest of the body cannot function . . . at least not as well. You and I were made to belong to God—that is the ultimate relationship—and then to a cluster of His people. The one thing that drives us to seek that state is our loneliness.

Loneliness is a gift not unlike pain. God wills for you and

me to be well physically until we die. That's His best plan. Sickness is not part of His best plan. If we step on a broken bottle at the beach, we feel pain. Pain gives us a message. It tells us to interrupt what we're doing and take care of that bleeding foot. Pain prevents us from continuing as though nothing had happened. We've got to stop and take care of whatever hurts so that we can continue to live. So as pain forces us to find healing, loneliness drives us to love and community and God.

There's no way to escape loneliness. The key is to use it constructively. Our Lord was totally human, though without sin. And being totally human, He was exactly like us in every way. As the ultimate Person He had ultimate loneliness. The New Testament tells us what He did with His loneliness. We read the account of His night of prayer in Gethsemane just before He was betrayed and arrested. He is at the very end of His earthly life, and He is saying two things in that final prayer (*see* Mark 14). He is feeling, first of all, cut off from God, not sure if He is really in God's will. To put it in today's language, He is saying, "Father, maybe I blew it. Maybe there was a fork in the road I missed, and now I'm headed for this valley of pain and humiliation and annihilation. Perhaps that wasn't what You planned for me. But even if it is Your will, Father, I'm not sure I can go through with it. It's too costly." It was a time of ultimate loneliness, and being totally human, Jesus couldn't escape it. But He had two options. He could either hide His loneliness and go off and pray alone or He could share it. He asked three of His disciples, Peter, James, and John, to join Him in His lonely vigil. He was able to say, "I'm lonely, I'm frightened. Will you three come and keep me company in this last few hours of my life?" They went, even though they kept falling asleep, and because of their account of that agonizing night, Jesus shared His loneliness with all of us.

Hazel and I have taken a number of groups to the Holy

Land in past years. As a kind of spiritual "voyeur," I'm always intrigued by what particular place, among those many holy places, turns people on. Gethsemane is certainly one of those places. *Gethsemane,* in Hebrew, simply means "olive press." There was an olive grove on the side of the hill, and there was an olive press in that grove. Jesus and the three disciples went out to an orchard that looked across the Kidron Valley to Jerusalem. There are still olive trees on that hillside—two of them at least two thousand years old. They have uncovered the remains of an old olive press. So it's almost certainly the garden where our Lord knelt and prayed that night. We pilgrims who visit there today are always moved, overwhelmed by the cost of God's love for us. We stand with tears flowing as we think of what happened— probably at that very spot. It is the place where Jesus let us know the depth of His suffering and the cost of His love for us. He shared His utter loneliness.

And Jesus says to us, "And this is My commandment, love one another as I have loved you" (*see* John 13:34). He has shown us how to deal with our loneliness. We can't escape it. But if we share it with someone else, God gives us the gift of community, of intimacy, and of love.

Some years ago I went to a meeting where Dr. Bob Pierce, founder of World Vision, was speaking. He was a worldwide evangelist and missionary, then near the end of his life. He had spent his life founding orphanages in Korea, rescuing children from death and starvation. As an evangelist he converted thousands of people all over the world. He was speaking to a small group, and most of us were in awe of what God had accomplished through this one committed man. But his message took us by surprise. He told us about an incident that had occurred one Christmas Eve when he was in Stockholm traveling with the Korean Children's Choir. He made a call home and talked to all the members of his family, wishing them a Merry Christmas. Finally, the youngest child got the phone. "Oh, Daddy," she said. "I wish I was an orphan so I could be with you on Christmas Eve." He told us, "My heart broke. And I say to you now that I'm not sure if I *was* in the will of the Lord all those years. I know God has used me—God uses whatever you give Him. But I'm still wondering if perhaps I did not have a prior commitment to my own family, my own children? Was it God's will for me to be away so much? I simply don't know." Somehow as he opened his heart to us and showed us the pain and uncertainty he had experienced, the Spirit of the Living Christ filled that room. As Bob Pierce shared his loneliness and confusion, we felt loved.

Do you want to live at this level? Suppose some Saturday night your pastor calls you to come over to the parsonage perhaps with two or three others. When you arrive he might say, "Come in, I hope you can spare the whole evening. I've got the coffeepot on. It's been a bad week for me. I really haven't prayed sincerely all week and haven't talked civilly to my wife for ten days. I'm mad at God. I hate myself. Tomorrow is Sunday. I'm supposed to preach and bring the Good News to God's people and I'm in no shape to do it. And so tonight I'm going to wrestle with God and see if He can find me again, put me in my right mind, and fill me one more time with the Spirit. I'm not sure that He can and I'm not sure that I'll let Him. I know He wants to, but it's one of those dark nights of the soul. Would you three friends simply keep me company? I'm terrified." Could you handle that kind of situation—accept that kind of pastor, one who doesn't always have it together? That's what the gift of loneliness is all about.

As you deal with your loneliness, I would urge you to remember three things: First, your loneliness is inevitable. You can't escape it. Accept it. Second, see it as God's gift to you. Were it not for loneliness, you and I would never reach out for God or for each other. New relationships are scary, but loneliness drives us to seek them. Finally, as you reach out to share the gift of loneliness with others, expect God to be there even as He was at Gethsemane. Christian community is loneliness shared with God and one another. You're not to make the faith journey alone. He gives us companions for the road.

CHAPTER SIX

How to Love Your Traveling Companions

J ESUS, on the occasion of His last supper with His disciples in the Upper Room, gave them a new commandment. They were celebrating the Passover, and it was a meal in which so many dramatic events happened. Jesus demonstrated servanthood by taking a towel and basin and washing the feet of the twelve. It was on this night that He revealed that Judas would betray Him and that He was to die. He instituted the breaking of bread and drinking of wine, the first communion. But on two separate occasions on this last night together, according to John's gospel, He gave them a new commandment to "love one another as I have loved you."

Early in this century, Henry Drummond, a Scottish scientist, wrote a small book which has probably sold close to fifty million copies. Its title is, *The Greatest Thing in the World,* and it is a book about love, an exposition of the thirteenth chapter of Paul's first letter to the Corinthians. Most of us would agree that love is the greatest thing in the world. I saw an ad in the paper recently that said, "Saleslady wanted who loves people, full or part-time." Any good salesperson has to love people, but it's a quality that's an asset in any job.

Freud revolutionized the psychological world with his theory that sex is the number-one human drive. Shortly afterward that premise was challenged by Alfred Adler, who believed that we are all motivated by the desire for power. But I think the need for love is a stronger drive than either of those. Your goal may be to be the most beautiful, the wisest, the richest, or the most powerful. But underlying that need is the desire for something that will make people love you.

When our city symphony hired a new conductor, he was interviewed by the local paper. He was asked how he handled the acclaim that came with the job. His answer was perceptive. It went something like this: "I'm not in demand because I'm such a marvelous person. It all comes with the job. Sometimes I wonder if I had to go to prison or endure some kind of disgrace, how many friends would still be there." I'll bet you've wondered about that a few times in the middle of a sleepless night. If you suddenly lost your respectability or even just the position of power you've attained, would you still be loved? It's an unsettling question.

Jesus understood that our need for love is infinite. That's the mark of God in us. He made us with a capacity for love that only He can satisfy. That's why so many of our relationships are, at best, unsatisfying. The lyrics of a popular song of some years back claim, "You always hurt the one you love," and those words strike a chord. No matter how much that other person means to you—your spouse, your parents, your child, your dear friend—he or she, being finite, does not have the capacity to love you sufficiently. We tend to believe either that the fault is ours or that there is a flaw in the other person. We turn on the people we love most because they can't seem to love us enough. How freeing to realize that God made us for Himself. Only He can fill that infinite capacity for love. As Saint Augustine said, "Our hearts are restless until they rest in Thee."

Assuming that we are committed to loving one another as He has loved us, as He commanded His disciples on that last dramatic evening, I still think we need a strategy of love. Central to that strategy is negotiability. The dictionary defines *negotiable* as "transferable from one person to another for value." Love must be acted out in ways that are transferable and of value to the person receiving it. All of us can think of too many examples of misguided, misplaced, and nonnegotiable kinds of love in the lives of people around us. The parents of John Hinckley, the young man who attempted to assassinate President Reagan, dearly loved their troubled son. Some of us saw that devastated father on the TV news tearfully saying, "I wish I could take my son's place. I take the blame. I love that boy." We can't doubt that father's love, but somehow his strategy for loving failed.

Most of us who have been parents have felt a sense of failure over a problem child at some time. We want so much to express the love that we feel in a negotiable way, a way perceived by that son or daughter as something of value. *Time* magazine did a feature on problem children in which Chris Moring, from the Georgia Mental Health Institute, is quoted on the need for an effective strategy of love: "Speaking of problem children, nothing works with everybody all the time, but there are very few cases in which some strategy does not work." There's no definitive book on "How to Love Problem Children." The Holy Spirit must prompt and guide us to find a way to love that problem child—and that problem parent or that problem spouse. The strategy of love keeps changing and it must be tailored to the needs of the object of our love.

It might be helpful to examine, first of all, what nonnegotiable love looks like. Nonnegotiable love is something that we enjoy giving, but which has no value to the other person. It meets our needs, not theirs. Advice giving could head the list. We don't listen to people; we just tell them what they ought to do. Advice giving puts us in a superior position and often takes the place of helping those other people to walk through their pain and find solutions that are their own. There's a little shop in Spokane, Washington, on an out-of-the-way side street, where for fifteen dollars you can talk to somebody for half an hour, someone who promises to listen to you without offering any advice. It's staffed by lay people only, and it is called "Let's Talk." People pay that fifteen dollars gladly and consider it a bargain because listeners are so rare.

Criticism is another form of nonnegotiable love. So many of us are programmed to criticize rather than affirm. My wife has been editing my books for over ten years, and I appreciate her enormously. But we've had a problem. I'd give her a chapter to read and she'd say something like, "This opening paragraph is really dull." I'd say, "Well, how was the chapter?" Usually there was a lot that she liked in the chapter, but she always started with the flaw. Finally, I said, "Please, if there's something of redeeming value, tell me about that first." Now, she might say, "I love the word you've used here in the last paragraph of your chapter. It's exactly right." She may go on to say the rest of the chapter is unexciting, but she's learning to begin with the positive. When she does, I somehow relax, and can even handle criticism.

I would put in this category of nonnegotiable love something we'll call total recall. Here's how it goes. When someone says, "My mother is in the hospital having surgery," we reply, "Oh, that reminds me of the time that my mother was in the hospital. I was just fifteen at the time, and it was serious gallbladder surgery, and her doctors said. . . ." And so on, and so on. Sound familiar? Friends, that's nonnegotiable love.

Our love is nonnegotiable when we make excuses for the other person. Believe me, we are giving something of no value. For those of us who are Christians, there are rules, implacable and unchangeable. We've got to remind the people we love about those rules when they're breaking them. The *Time* article I mentioned earlier talked about this kind of tough love. It cited the case of an eighteen-year-old boy who was arrested for mugging. His wealthy mother tried to hire a psychiatrist to testify in court that the boy was really mentally ill. He threw her out of the office. The young man needed to learn that there are rules, and consequences for breaking them.

I'd put sympathy on that list of ways to love nonnegotiably. Sympathy is demeaning. Jesus never gave people sympathy. He wept with those who wept; He laughed with those who laughed. But He never said, "Oh, you poor thing. Isn't it awful?" We are not to encourage people who are feeling sorry for themselves. Rather, we are to help them examine the possibilities for changing their situation or their attitude.

When Mother Teresa received a degree at Georgetown University, she said, among other things, "The poor don't need bread, they need love." That's a little strong. I happen to think the poor need bread *and* love. But I understand her point. To give bread without love is to rob people of their dignity. Sympathy alone can prompt an act of benevolence, but empathy requires that we stand with that person in need, offering love and friendship.

Jesus is our model for negotiable love. He is God's negotiable love for you and me. He said, "Greater love has no man than this, that a man lay down his life for his friends. You are my friends" (John 15:13, 14 RSV). He gave His life for us while we were totally undeserving. He asks us to give that same love to one another, deserving or not.

Jesus loved those close at hand. They were primary tar-

gets for His love, those twelve who traveled with Him, and
then the larger circle of men and women who followed Him
and His teachings. I can think of some people who have almost literally stepped over the bodies of family and friends
to go out and do a great missionary work in the world. You
may know people like that. They care for the poor, they are
heads of missions, they give their time and energy for the
homeless and hungry; but the people in their immediate circle are neglected and of no account. Yes, we need to go into
the uttermost parts of the world, but we are to begin, as
Jesus did, with the people around us.

Negotiable love is tangible. Remember when the blind
man came to Jesus for healing, and the disciples tried to
make His situation the subject of a theological discussion?
Why was this man blind? Was it the result of his sin, or the
sin of his parents? Jesus reprimanded them, saying in effect,
"It doesn't matter. Let's heal him." Our love may take the
form of money, time, prayer, work, but it must be something
of tangible value.

In simple terms, negotiable love is love that is meaningful
for the other person. In the first year that Hazel and I were
married, I remember a particular day when I was feeling
depressed. She was eight months pregnant, we were students
at Princeton and exams loomed ahead, and we had no call
as yet to a church. It was a miserable, rainy Saturday morning, and I was amazed when she suddenly suggested we go
fishing. I said, "You're kidding." I'm a fishing nut, but that's
not exactly her thing. Nevertheless, we headed for Point
Pleasant, rented a little boat, and headed out to sea in driz-
zling rain and we fished. I tell you, I felt loved. At a time
when I needed it most, she expressed love in terms that I
could understand.

I heard about a little girl who came running into the class-
room during recess to find her teacher. "Teacher," she said,

"there are two boys out in the schoolyard fighting, and I think the one on the bottom would like to see you very much." That's negotiable love—when you're getting clobbered and somebody comes to peel off the guy on top of you.

Negotiable love never lays blame. Jesus says to the woman caught in adultery, "Neither do I condemn you, but go and sin no more" (*see* John 8:3–11). As we said, God has given us rules and we're supposed to keep them. But, through Christ's death on the cross, there is forgiveness.

Negotiable love is marked by vulnerability. We need to say to those around us, "I need you." "Help me." "I won't make it without you." Again, our role model is Jesus, who asked the Samaritan woman for water; Zacchaeus for a meal; Peter, James, and John to sit up all night with Him at Gethsemane and share the most agonizing hours of His life.

Finally, negotiable love affirms. Our love conveys, "I trust you; you can do it." Jesus sent the disciples out two by two to heal the sick, to proclaim the Kingdom, to cast out demons. They were hesitant, fearful, and He believed in them. So He sends us all. We are to go into all the world and, as He says in those words, repeated twice in the Upper Room that fateful night, we are to "love each other as I have loved you."

CHAPTER SEVEN

The Road to Cana

JESUS PERFORMED His very first miracle at a wedding in Cana. We assume He wanted it to be a joyous and memorable day, not just for the bride and groom but for all the guests. Most of us have been on the Cana Road on more than one occasion—on the way to a wedding. What is it we bring to those events in terms of our own attitudes and expectations, be it the wedding of friends or relatives or, more particularly, our own?

As a pastor, I do a good deal of marriage counseling. I often wish that I could delay that counseling until three months after the wedding. It's hard to suggest to a couple, starry-eyed and infatuated with each other, that there will be problems and pitfalls ahead. They just don't believe it. I think they'd be better equipped some three months into the marriage to understand some of the things I'm talking about.

Living happily ever after is not exactly the norm, according to "Dear Abby," counselor to the nation. Certainly she is in touch with more people volume-wise than almost anyone else, except perhaps her sister, Ann Landers. She claims that for every twenty marriages, one is fulfilled, four are okay, ten are unfulfilled, and five are miserable. Do you believe those statistics? Is that an accurate assessment of the married couples you know? Further, how do those statistics make you feel? Relieved that you're not the only suffering one? Or, you may be amazed and thinking, "It can't be true. I'm so fulfilled and most of my married friends seem so happy." I doubt that many of us could say that.

It's easy to be cynical about marriage. Marriage, as an institution, gets a lot of bad press. There are the jokes—the man who says, "If my wife really loved me, she wouldn't have married me." Susie Sutton says, "Marriage really has some good sides to it. It teaches forbearance, patience, self-restraint, and many other qualities you wouldn't need if you'd stayed single." Then there's that very old wheeze about an eighty-five-year-old man who was asked the reason for his remarkable health. He said, "My wife and I agreed sixty years ago that if she was mad at me, she'd tell me and get it off her chest. If I was mad at her, I would take a walk. I attribute my good health to the fact that I have led, for the most part, an outdoor life."

Unfortunately, there are plenty of reasons for feeling cynical about marriage. But, we are seeing in our decade a new optimism about and affirmation of this ancient institution. Sex without commitment is not as prevalent. Those who wrote about "open marriage" a decade or more ago are saying now that it doesn't work. It seems the old biblical values of chastity, monogamy, and fidelity are being rediscovered. We're told that people are marrying later in life. I'm delighted to hear that. Statistics prove that the longer you wait to marry, the better your chances are of having a lasting marriage. That makes sense to me. If you marry before you even know who you are, hoping marriage will define that for you, you're going to have problems. If you've had time to discover yourself, you have a better chance of understanding what to look for in a life partner.

Jesus' views of marriage are all too clear and, in regard to divorce (*see* Matthew 19:8, 9), uncomfortably narrow. But let's remember that God is the author of romance. He created them "male and female" with the idea in mind that they would marry and become one flesh, one spirit, one mind. God planned the whole mysterious process. Divorce is the severing of a living entity, separation of flesh from flesh. It's not the breakup of an arrangement between roommates or even lovers.

In Christian marriage, we believe that "these two shall be one" and in those verses in Matthew, Jesus tells the Pharisees that Moses permitted divorce "because of your hardness of heart." The Jews of those days were looking for loopholes in God's exact laws, and we still do that. The movie *Divorce Italian Style* addressed that problem. Because Italy is largely a Roman Catholic country, divorce is not easily obtained. On the other hand, the law deals leniently with those people who, in a fit of passion, kill their spouse. Ergo—divorce Italian style.

A Roman Catholic lawyer has written a self-help book for Catholics on the subject of annulment. The Catholic Church has always permitted divorce on approved grounds, but their view of Scripture precludes remarriage. That's why people prefer the annulment procedure. If the church annuls your marriage, you can be married again because you were never actually married the first time. The book advises Catholics on how to obtain an annulment in the church's courts. It is a commentary on our times that in 1969, the Roman Catholic Church in America annulled 350 marriages. In 1983, 52,000 annulments were granted. All of which suggests that for a lot of people there are problems in marriage.

Let's think about some of them for a moment. From my perspective as a pastor-counselor, one of the commonest is false expectations. They call it the "Cinderella Syndrome," and I mentioned it in an earlier chapter. Cinderella marries the prince and lives happily ever after. We plant the idea in children's minds that if life is tough, disappointing, not exciting, it will all change when Prince or Princess Charming comes along. They are to live happily ever after.

The point is that God never intended that your life would be fulfilled by marriage. Marriage cannot take His place. Your spouse is a gift, but he or she cannot fulfill all your needs. God alone is the source of our ultimate joy and satisfaction.

For most of us, there is a second problem, almost as deadly—a power struggle. All of us are power players. It's not what we do, but who decides what we do. A man elected to Congress was asked by a journalist, "Sir, when you go to Washington, will you give in to the powerful forces that everyone knows control you?" He replied, "I would thank you to refer only to my job and leave my wife out of it."

A number of the people I counsel have problems because they are married to a nonbeliever. This is an enormous obstacle to a happy marriage. It's not that Christians are necessarily better than other people morally or religiously. But if Jesus Christ is the number one Person and focus of your life, and you marry somebody who says, "Jesus who? God who?" you are in for heartache. How can you live happily together when the most important thing in your life is not shared by your partner? The Bible says unequivocally that believers should not marry unbelievers. However, we also read that if you're married to an unbeliever when you become a Christian, you are to stay in that relationship, with the promise that your spouse will be saved by your faith.

About one hundred years ago, William Rathbone, a Quaker, was dismissed from his congregation for marrying a Unitarian. He was subsequently restored to membership, and on that occasion he made this declaration: "Out of courtesy to my wife, I cannot say I repent of having married her, but I would never do it again." The Quakers took this biblical injunction about marriage to an unbeliever very seriously.

Loss of identity is another common problem. In marriage, we are to become one flesh, but that does not mean becoming one personality. The symbiotic relationship, where one person finds his or her identity in the other, is not what God has in mind. Let's remember, everybody is single. We go through life's turnstiles one by one. You're born alone. You die alone. If you're fortunate, you have the privilege of sharing your life with a lover, a friend, a spouse—but ultimately in every crucial decision you are alone. In a good marriage, each partner will become more of a person, stronger, freer, more fulfilled.

Two elderly Quaker ladies, lifelong spinsters, were asked why they had never married. One said, "Because it takes a mighty good husband to be better than none." The other was equally content with her state. "I may have missed the best," she said, "but I certainly escaped the worst." The point is, marriage can make you less of a person—dependent, cautious, closed to new ideas, experiences, and relationships. It *should* do just the opposite. You ought to be free to be all God meant you to be, because of the love and support of your partner.

At least half of our marriage problems are the result of bad communication. Conversely, perhaps the other half are caused by clear communication. Your spouse may be communicating exactly how he or she feels about you, and it's far from positive.

I happen to believe that openness is crucial to a good, healthy marriage. The last verse of Genesis 2 reports that Adam and Eve, "were naked and they were not ashamed." That's the kind of openness and guilelessness that Jesus

Christ came to restore in us. We are sinful men and women, but by His grace we are forgiven, and can therefore reveal ourselves intimately before at least one other person—our spouse. Secrets destroy intimacy.

I don't even mean big secrets like robbing a bank or having an affair. I am talking about the little secrets you begin to squirrel away. You begin building walls lest the person you live with discover those secrets. Fear builds; and psychologists tell us fear kills spontaneity. Marriage deteriorates into boring routine. The marriage God intends for us means living together naked and unashamed with no secrets.

Those are just a few of the problems, but let's consider some of the positive things we can do, either to heal a troubled marriage or to improve a good one.

Begin by taking responsibility. I suggest you pray, "Lord, change this marriage, beginning with me." Don't blame your spouse for all that's wrong. The question I always ask people in a marriage-counseling situation is, "Do you want this marriage to work?" If they say yes, I tell them God has a way to make it work if they're willing to say, "Lord, change this marriage, beginning with me." If you don't want the marriage to continue, no amount of counseling will help and even God Himself can't help.

Have realistic expectations of your spouse. Don't lay on your partner that he or she is the end all and be all for you. If you're at a breaking point, choose not to be angry for thirty days. Nobody makes us angry. We choose to be angry. We can choose not to be angry for at least thirty days. That gives us a chance to look at our marriage in a new way.

Give negotiable love. Plan a strategy to demonstrate to your spouse, "I love you and God loves you." That means a whole variety of things, depending on the couple. Where is the battleground? Over money, sex, housekeeping, the use of time? What is the area in which you could prove your love tangibly and unmistakably? Begin to do that and ask God's help in doing it.

Fight fair. Fighting, as traumatic as it is, is preferable to bottling up your anger. When a couple comes to me claiming, "We've never had a cross word in thirty years," I start to worry about them. If you're at all in touch with your feelings, you're going to experience anger and resentment and you need to express it. But try to avoid the words *never* and *always*. Don't say, "You know, you *never* care about me, you *never* take the garbage out," or, "You're *always* late," "You *always* put me down." Instead, stick to how you feel. "This is how I feel when you do that—minimized, hurt, discounted." No one can argue with your feelings. Choose a good time and place to fight: As you leave for church at 10:30 Sunday morning is not a good time or place.

Have a sense of humor. Try to laugh at yourself. Tommy Lasorda, one of the great baseball coaches of all time, claims his wife accused him of loving baseball more than he loved her. He said, "You know, I think you're right. But I love you more than football and basketball." A little humor can defuse a lot of anger.

Be priests to each other. Make an effort to channel the miraculous love of God to your spouse. At the end of a day that may have been full of disappointment or difficulty, your job is to greet your partner as his or her priest: "Honey, God told me to tell you you are loved."

Jesus turned the water into wine at that wedding in Cana. He wanted a happy occasion to be even more joyous. It seems to me He wants to do that for all of us who are married—to take the ordinary, sometimes dull, day-to-day relationships of your marriage and mine and make it all a joyous celebration.

CHAPTER EIGHT

The Road to Your Place

J ESUS SAID, "In my Father's house are many rooms; I go to prepare a place for you." He did not say, "In my Father's house there is a great dormitory. You'll have your own bed, but you'll all be living under one roof, a great summer camp in the sky." Jesus promised to prepare a different place for each one of us, and I believe that reveals a profound, spiritual truth about life and what it's meant to be. One of the major battles being waged between the forces of darkness and the forces of light centers on conformity. God's creative Spirit has made every snowflake different, every leaf unique. How much more are we, made in His image, to be the unrepeatable miracle that He dreamed of when He first thought of us eons ago?

The adversary's goal is the reverse of that. He wants us to conform, to be like everybody else. We are to look alike, smell alike, sing alike, and sound alike. If he can turn us as a people into that kind of monotonous, monolithic mass, he will have the victory. God went to a great deal of trouble through His Son's life and death and Resurrection to set us free to be ourselves to His glory and honor. As those unique people, each of us requires a different environment. We have different comfort zones. Sometimes when I'm conducting a workshop, I ask the participants to name their favorite room in the house. The variety of answers is remarkable. One will say, "I love the kitchen. I like to cook, or just to be around cooking. I like the aroma of food. The kitchen is the soul of the house." Some mention the library, where books are kept, where you can sit and read on a rainy day. Some say it's the bedroom. They like the feeling of privacy. You can close the door and relax or sleep, or be alone with God.

Some actually say the bathroom. There's the appeal of an invigorating shower or hot tub full of bubbles, or, in some cases, one place to shut the door and be alone for a few minutes away from little people and their demands. The dining room is a favorite of many. They mention leisurely dinners around the table and interesting conversation, long after the food is gone. I've had people choose the basement. "That's where I have my workshop or my crafts." In some cases, it's the garage, for a variety of reasons. One woman chose it because she's a gardener and that's where she keeps her gardening equipment.

I think most of us have a particular geography as well, through which if we had our own way, our faith journey would take us—physical surroundings that seem to speak to our needs. If you had to choose one place to live out the rest of your life, where would it be? Do you like the mountains, the forest, the ocean, the plains, the desert? Do you love the city, the country, an island? Ruth and Billy Graham had an opportunity to make such a choice. With his peripatetic ministry, they were free to make their home almost any place. Billy, we're told, is an ocean person. He loves the sand, the seashore, and the vast expanse of water. Ruth, on the other hand, is a mountain person. The Grahams opted to live in the mountains. I assume that's because Ruth is at home far more than Billy. Most of us are so committed to jobs and relationships that we don't have that sort of open-ended choice. Nevertheless, there are those special places for all of us where we feel most ourselves, where the geography ministers to something deep in our souls.

Even church architecture is a deeply personal matter in the way it meets our needs. You may visit a particular church building and immediately feel at home and in communion with God. That same building may do nothing at all for others. Church buildings can evoke deep memories and emotions—some that go back to what Carl Jung would call our group unconscious. I grew up in a great Gothic church, a style of architecture from northern Europe. It is an attempt to duplicate the experience of being in a great, tall pine forest, the kind of place where those early European tribes worshipped before there were buildings.

The Byzantine churches of the Mediterranean area are symbolic of the caves that were used for worshipping the gods eons ago. Those churches are fairly low and have all sorts of niches and alcoves. That feels exactly right to part of the Christian family. I'm partial to the New England meetinghouse. Their premise is that a church ought to remind you of home. Large or small, these churches look like houses with clear windows and simple architecture. There is a theology of church architecture, and I think any church committee planning a new building ought to ask, "What can we build that will represent architecturally what we believe about God and who we see ourselves to be as His people?"

There is, perhaps, no more obvious an extension of your own soul than your home. Whether it is an apartment, a house, a trailer, or even a houseboat, where you live is an extension of the inner you. When I come into your home, I immediately have a deeper understanding of who you are. The colors of the walls, the artwork or lack of it, the starkness or clutter, all are a reflection of the dweller. That explains why most people who suffer a burglary consider it such a violation, almost in a category with rape. When somebody comes into your home uninvited and goes through your personal possessions, they trample on your soul.

A couple of dear friends of mine went together all through college and for three or four years afterward. They loved each other, but marriage plans never seemed to work out. One day walking on the beach, he raised a question, "Tell me, honey, where do you see yourself living in ten years?" She said, "I'd like to be on an island in the San Juans, living in a log cabin we built ourselves and raising horses." He was stunned. "I've always seen myself living in New York City in some loft, writing books." That conversation was the end of the relationship. When you try to join the architecture of two souls, you need compatible pieces.

The architecture and ambience of your life are shaping forces, and so is your geographic location. Some people hate small towns and others love them. For some, a small town is a place where you are secure. Whatever you do and however you fail, you're accepted. Others feel trapped in a small town. Whatever they accomplish, they never outgrow the label the town has given them. The same town represents safety for some and a dead end for others. My wife is from a small town where I was a student minister. I tell her that if I become president of the United States or the number-one criminal on the FBI's most-wanted list, it wouldn't change who I am in that town. I would still be the guy who married George Fischer's youngest daughter. Would that make you feel comfortable, or panicky?

A study was made at Grace Hospital in New Haven, Connecticut, some years ago to try to determine ideal therapeutic surroundings for people who suffer with emotional and mental problems. They discovered there is no such thing. Some people recover faster in the shared intimacy of the dormitory, where there is a sense of community. Others are threatened by that life-style and need a private room and freedom to come and go at will, to choose to be part of a group or to retreat.

Winston Churchill said, "We shape our buildings and thereafter they shape us." We erect a building—a church, an office building, a new home—and we are molded by that structure, its form and its ambience. What a ministry architects have! Before they design your house, it's imperative that they spend time with you to get to know something about you and the environment you want to create to be the person you want to be.

Marion Diamond is a professor at the University of California at Berkeley. She has done a study of rats proving that the design of their cage can increase physical brain growth. If you put rats in an ideal environment with plenty of space, lots of diversions, and companionship, measurable, discernible brain growth takes place even into old age. Other rats on the same diet but with crowded conditions, no stimulation, and no company do not experience this brain growth. The conclusion is that environment is a factor in brain growth for rats, and, who knows, it might be for human beings as well.

There have been studies done recently on the effect on humans of light and sunshine. Deprived of a sufficient amount of these, the hormone melatonin increases, resulting in depression in certain people. I recently met a man on a plane who had moved with his wife to Seattle a year ago. "We're moving out," he said. "She's going bananas with all this rain." Perhaps her problem is the increased melatonin, as studies suggest. At any rate, it appears that some people can benefit from locating in an area where they get more light and sunshine.

What kind of ambience do you need to feel God's presence? I have friends who tell me God speaks most clearly while they're jogging. I think, for a lot of people, some sort of physical exertion—walking, biking, sailing, swimming, or whatever—heightens their awareness of God. Others need a quiet and relaxed activity to feel open to God—gardening, sewing, sitting in a hot tub. The important thing is to discover the place where God has access to you. It may be unlike anyone else's place.

Jesus says, "I go to prepare a place for you" (John 14:2 RSV), but by faith we can prepare one now for ourselves—a place that reflects our uniqueness, and that is conducive to communing with God. Some people seem to find that "right place" intuitively. When our singles pastor joined the staff, he had to start house hunting. His wife, Eileen, said, "I'm looking for the right place." The first time she saw a certain old, blue Victorian house, she said, "This is it."

Ambience and architecture are important, but the right place can have a great deal to do with relationships and lifestyles and even philosophical compatibility. A Shanghai newspaper ran a story last year about a soon-to-graduate medical student who drowned saving an elderly peasant who had fallen into a canal. The story appeared on the front page and prompted sixteen hundred indignant letters. The bottom line of them all was this: What a waste! With all the money the state had spent to train this student, why would he throw his life away to save some old peasant? Personally, I would hate to live in a place where life is measured in those terms. Whatever our flaws here in America, we are united in our admiration for those capable of bravery and self-sacrifice.

Our journey unfolds as we put God at the center, live with a community of people who care about Him, and find a place where we can be all that we were meant to be. However, I am well aware that the place for refuge on the journey is a given for all too many. Those people have not the luxury of the kinds of choices and options we've discussed here. They are to be found in the poverty pockets of our own land as well as in nations such as China, Russia, Poland, and South Africa, to name just a few. For those, Jesus' promise to "prepare a place" must be especially meaningful. We can only imagine their longing for the kind of place that will ultimately meet all their needs—physical, spiritual, and even aesthetic.

The rest of us, those with the political and/or economic freedom to exercise our options, need to do so that we might maximize our potential for faith and witness. Find that right place. It will heighten the journey.

CHAPTER NINE

The Roads Where Jesus Walked

SOME YEARS AGO I had the privilege of being invited to be
the guest speaker for a Methodist church in Bermuda celebrating its 200th birthday. There were week-long services
climaxed by a great birthday service on Sunday. The governor of the island attended, sitting in a reserved pew, com-
plete with all his entourage. I preached on the first chapter
of Mark, the account of Jesus walking by the sea and calling
the first disciples.

At the door after the service, the governor was the first
one out. This elegant, mustachioed gentleman shook my
hand and looked at me somewhat wistfully. "Thank you,
pastor, for the message. If only what you were saying about
following Jesus was possible." With that, he darted out the
door. I've never forgotten his poignant comment.

In the early part of this century, Charles Sheldon wrote a
book, *In His Steps*. It enjoyed great popularity, perhaps because that idea has captured the imaginations of people of
all ages for the last two thousand years. Is it possible to follow in Jesus' steps, and if so, how do you do it? One of the
earliest pilgrims was the mother of Constantine, the first
Christian ruler of the Roman Empire. This devout lady set

off for the Holy Land and embarked on the first archaeological exploration for the holy places. It was she who designated the exact spot of Jesus' birth and the location of the tomb where the Resurrection took place. Churches were, of course, immediately built on all the holy sites.

Much later on, the Crusaders followed the steps of Jesus, leading armies to Palestine to wrest all these holy places from the Turks. This was a tragic time, as we all know. There was even a Children's Crusade, in which tens of thousands were slaughtered. It was a terrible chapter in the church's history. In the ensuing centuries, various holy orders have been established by monks and nuns who wanted to live and work in the place where Jesus walked.

In the earliest part of our century there was a quest for the historical Jesus, led by no less a person than Albert Schweitzer, the great missionary doctor. The rationale was to get past the Jesus of theology, the Jesus we sing about, the Jesus of the Bible, and to try to find exactly who this person was historically.

Then there have been the streams of individual pilgrims over the years who want so much to see the places where Jesus walked and taught, the city where He was born, and the tomb from which He arose. All of this helps us understand why the book, *In His Steps,* struck such a nerve for Christians. Actually, the thesis of the book is that we need not go to the Holy Land: We can walk "In His Steps" in our own city. It's the story of a dwindling, apathetic congregation who decide to live every day in every situation by asking, "What would Jesus do if He were here?"

Because of this new strategy, the church experiences an awakening. Well, it all sounds great, but it's theologically unsound. When you ask, "What would Jesus do?" it means you don't believe He is here. The truth is that by the power of the Holy Spirit, He is here. He is with you and me as we go through our day-to-day routines. Our prayer should be, "Lord, You're here. What do You want *me* to do?"

Going to the Holy Land to walk where Jesus walked is such an attractive idea, but it is largely impossible. It was only on my most recent trip to Israel that I learned exactly how the Romans had devastated Jerusalem after Jesus' death and Resurrection. I assumed they had simply torn down all the buildings and walls. According to archaeologists, however, they razed the city, as though with a bulldozer. When Jerusalem was rebuilt, there were few clues as to where any of the original buildings had stood. I'm convinced that God's hand was in that. I think He used those circumstances to insure that no one could say with certainty, "The Upper Room was here," or "The Crucifixion took place over there." We can be reasonably certain about some of those sites, but there is lots of room for doubts and questions.

The four gospels are similarly imprecise in terms of the historical details we'd like to have. God chose four very different people to write these accounts: Matthew, Mark, Luke, and John. Each wrote with a different frame of reference and to a different audience. They are full of details about times and places, people and conversations. But, how is it that not one of them gives a clue about Jesus' appearance? We don't know if He was tall or short, fat or thin. Did He have an athletic build or was He frail? What about His voice—loud or soft, low or high? Not once do they write, "The tall, slender Jesus came down from the mountain. . . ." Or, "The little, rotund Jesus came up the road." Again, it seems to be God's best plan. We are not to worship places or physical characteristics. The events are not to be obscured by those kinds of details.

It's just as hard to come up with a psychological profile of Jesus. What motives did He have for saying some of the things the gospels record? He cautioned one man whom He had healed to "tell no one." The man couldn't wait to tell the whole town. Did Jesus know he would do that? He warned His disciples about the difficulty of following Him, of the hardships they would have to endure. "The foxes have holes . . ." (Matthew 8:20). They followed Him anyway, but was the warning just a clever ploy? Then there's Zacchaeus. Of all the people in Jericho, why did Jesus pick him to spend time with? Over lunch this man's life was turned around and he gave away half his goods to the poor.

But why Zacchaeus in the first place? Was it because he was the most unlikely person in town, and Jesus could demonstrate the mighty power of God, or did He know instinctively that this was the one man who was ready to hear about the Kingdom of God? The Lazarus story is puzzling. Jesus heard that His beloved friend, brother of Mary and Martha, was dying, and yet He did not go to him immediately. By the time He got to Bethany, a suburb of Jerusalem, Lazarus had been dead four days. We read that He wept, and yet He also said, "I have come to show the power of God," and He raised His friend from the dead. It seems impossible to understand the intricate workings of Jesus' mind.

Most of our hymnbooks contain that sentimental hymn that goes, "I think when I read that sweet story of old, When Jesus was here among men, How He called little children like lambs to His fold. I should like to have been with Him then." It's fun to sing, but it's sentimental nonsense. Nobody misunderstood Jesus more than those who were with Him then. Obstinately and repeatedly, they didn't understand Him. Throughout His ministry, He reproved them with words such as, "Have I been so long with you, and yet have you not known me?" Or, "Get thee behind me, Satan." They simply didn't understand Jesus. But we need not mope about not having been with Him then. By the coming of the

Spirit at Pentecost, we have intimacy available to us that those who were with Him in the flesh did not have.

We may think we can "walk in Jesus' steps" to a successful and triumphant life. The Old Testament message was that if you are really walking in God's steps, you'll be blessed with health and wealth and many children. That same gospel is preached today, especially on television: If you follow Jesus, your life will overflow with material blessings and worldly success. However, Jesus' three-year ministry was not a success story. He began in His hometown, reading the Scripture in His home synagogue, and His hearers were mad enough to want to kill Him. They took Him out to the nearest hill, determined to throw Him off, and we can imagine what they were saying: "This is Mary and Joseph's oldest son. Who does He think He is, claiming that He is the fulfillment of the Old Testament prophecy?" In my own case, if they had wanted to kill me after my first sermon in my first church, I think I would have gotten the message that maybe I should be doing something other than preaching. I'm conditioned to success, not failure.

Jesus was undeterred. He moved immediately down to Capernaum beside the sea and preached and taught and healed with tremendous results. He called the disciples and they dropped everything—business, family ties, friends—and came. He healed the sick. We could say His waiting room was full all the time, and He had a 100 percent rate of cure. Unbelievable. In the midst of all this healing success, He left town to go into the hills alone. The twelve protested, of course, "Wait a minute. You can't go. You're a real success in this town." He didn't come to be a successful healer or teacher. He came to proclaim the Kingdom. Success and failure were incidental.

It seems to me the key to walking in Jesus' steps is not to ask, "Where did He walk?" The real question is, "Why?"

And that has nothing to do with success or failure. He had a commission. He was God's Messiah. The marks of any authentic pilgrimage are that we are pursuing a vision beyond this life. This earth is not our home. A comfortable life amid a loving family is not our ultimate goal. A successful job or profession is not what we're called to do. We are pilgrims just passing through, and, along the road, God gives us jobs to do. That's the key to walking in Jesus' steps.

I had an enlightening insight the last time I was in Israel. My guide arranged to have us stop at a little Jewish cemetery. I confess I was a little disgruntled. I thought, "Good grief! I didn't come all the way to Israel to see some obscure Jewish cemetery!" In the cemetery is one special tomb marking the grave of a woman named Rachel who died at age forty. She came to Israel late in life and had to learn Hebrew, but eventually she became the new state's official poetess. Visitors to her grave leave stones there as calling cards. It is a holy place. It seems she wrote many of her poems in that lovely spot, on the shores of the Sea of Galilee with Mount Nebo in the distance. You may remember that Nebo is where Moses died. He was not allowed to enter the Promised Land. One of her poems appears on her tombstone, and in it she writes that "everyone has a Nebo."

My reaction was, "Oh, would that everyone had a Nebo." That's what walking in the steps of Jesus is all about: to have a dream so big, you die perhaps never seeing it fulfilled. Think about Moses. He led those ungrateful Israelites for forty years and finally, after a new generation was born, and they were about to enter the Promised Land, he died on the threshold. Nebo represents his unfulfilled dream. Even Jesus, in His earthly life, never saw the Kingdom that we are a part of right now. He came not to heal the sick or take care of the poor or visit those in prison, though He did all that.

He came to proclaim the Kingdom. He died saying, "My God, why have you forsaken me?"

God made a promise to Abraham. If he would leave Ur of the Chaldees, secure and familiar, and start off on a perilous journey, he would be the father of a great nation, as many as the sands on the seashore. He died the father of one child, and that's all. He never saw the Israelite nation. David was promised a holy city, and he was not permitted to build the temple. Stephen, the first Christian martyr, died with his eyes on that heavenly vision, the Kingdom of God. As he was stoned, he prayed for his murderers.

Tradition tells us that the eleven apostles (Judas died by his own hand) were all crucified or killed for their faith. They never saw the fulfillment of the Kingdom they came to proclaim. John was exiled to Patmos, one of the most desolate places in the world, then or now. John, an old man dying in exile, wrote that he saw "a new heaven and a new earth." He saw it only in his mind. The dream, at that time, was largely unfulfilled.

Martin Luther King was leader and spokesman of the civil rights movement of the sixties. I'll never forget seeing him on television speaking on the mall in Washington to a huge crowd, with that moving rhetoric, "I have a dream." He was assassinated before he ever saw even the degree of equality or opportunity for black people that we take for granted today. His dream was unfulfilled.

Jonathan Edwards, the famous preacher of the eighteenth century, had a dream. Those were terrible times in our country, of immorality and rampant atheism. Edwards wrote in his journal: "Resolve that every man should live to the glory of God. Resolve, that whether others do this or not, I will." His eyes were fixed on a vision beyond what other people did, and because of that he became the center of a great awakening. The fires of revival blazed all over New England and people were converted in great numbers.

Jonathan Edwards died in 1758. His grandson, Timothy Dwight, became the president of Yale in 1795. Cycles come and go and the country had regressed back to immorality and unbelief. When Dwight assumed the presidency there was one Christian in the freshman class, two in the sophomore class, none in the junior class, and eight or nine in the senior class. The campus church had dwindled to two members. Dwight understood that he was not called simply to be a successful college president. Some seven or eight years later, one of Dwight's instructors wrote a letter home to his mother in which he said, "It would delight your heart to see how the trophies of the cross are multiplied in this institution. Yale College is a little temple."

Most of us have read the story of Marie Regianti, a thirty-four-year-old devout Catholic. Her early life was tragic. A battered wife, she had divorced her husband and was struggling to raise her two children alone. Eventually she got a well-paying and secure job, working for the governor of Tennessee. Before long, she realized he was asking her to do some shady things, to help parole prisoners who were guilty and a menace to society, but who had bribed the governor. Her friends all counseled her to go along with it. "Listen, Marie, you've got nothing to gain, everything to lose. You're a single parent and you can finally take care of your kids and relax. That's his problem." She couldn't. Her eyes were fixed on something beyond the immediate job and her own success. She exposed the whole situation and the governor is now in jail. She was motivated by a vision of right and justice that made her own personal interests seem petty.

Jesus said to His disciples by the Sea of Galilee, and He says to you and me, "Follow me." How do we follow in His steps? We need not go to Israel. We can be pilgrims where we are. We can have a dream to make our city the Holy City. Beyond that, we have our eyes on a city whose builder and maker is God. We may give our life to a cause that we'll never see fulfilled, but the calling is beyond success or failure.

Sometimes our dreams are too small. I talked to a man recently who always feared that when he retired, his pension wouldn't be big enough to enable him to keep his own home and live comfortably. He's still in his own home and he is financially secure. He plays golf every day and has a wife who loves him. His health is good. I said, "John, what is it you want that you don't have?" "Nothing," was the response. "Then, why is it you can't sleep at night? Your wife tells me you're up at two o'clock in the morning walking around the house. What's the trouble?" He wanted to be a success and he was, but perhaps his dream wasn't big enough.

Jesus met all sorts of people when He traveled the roads of Galilee. Some He taught and some He healed and to those special twelve men He said, "Follow me." He is still asking us to do that. When you're on the road with Jesus, don't settle for the next hill. Go all the way. His dreams for you are invariably bigger than your own.

CHAPTER TEN

Handling the Roadblocks

Many of us tend to think that our feelings often constitute a major roadblock on the faith road. We assume that God would have us be unruffled and docile servants, never giving vent to all the surging passions and feelings of which we're capable.

When you hear the word *feelings,* what is the first emotion that comes to your mind? Is it joy and gladness, or horror and dread? Perhaps you think of grief first of all. I'm always struck by those Israeli or Palestinian families we see on television mourning their dead. They scream and rant and rave. They really know how to express grief. Many of us more rigid types envy people with that capacity. You may associate feelings with rage and hatred, or you may think of love in all its expressions. You may associate feelings with compassion or passion, particularly sexual passion. Perhaps, for you, the word *feelings* is associated with hysteria, being out of control. That's especially likely if you've witnessed some family member who is subject to alcoholic rages or depression or hysterical outbursts.

Contrary to much Christian teaching, there are no good or bad feelings. Some of us grew up in churches where we were encouraged to have only "good" feelings and to hide or ignore the "bad" ones. But, of course, feelings are amoral.

We are judged by our actions, not by our feelings. We can't always control our feelings, but, with God's help, we can control our actions. We need not feel guilty about negative feelings.

As Christians, we believe Jesus was capable of deep feelings. He was sinless. Even His enemies could find no fault in Him, had no legitimate charges in terms of His conduct. But throughout the gospels, we find Him expressing all kinds of emotions—anger, frustration, disappointment, loneliness, plus positive feelings such as joy, peace, love, and all the rest. Everything you have ever felt, good or bad, He also felt.

Both Mark's and Matthew's Gospels recount the story of the fig tree. What a human picture of Jesus that episode paints. He was walking along the road, tired and hungry. There were no fast-food chains in Israel in those days, providing Big Macs or Kentucky Fried Chicken. But Jesus spied a fig tree in leaf, and assumed there would be ripe figs to eat, even though, according to Mark, it was not the season for figs. When He found no figs, He cursed the fig tree. "May no one ever eat fruit from you again." When the disciples passed by the next morning, the tree had withered away to its roots. At best, we have to say that's a display of ill temper.

On the other hand, His rage against the moneychangers in the temple is an example of justifiable anger. He found vendors in God's house making money on God's people and He was furious. John's Gospel records the scene vividly, leaving no doubt about what Jesus was feeling. He made a whip of cords and drove them out of the temple, along with the sheep and oxen. He poured out the coins and overturned their tables. He literally "threw the rascals out."

In the story of the man with the withered hand, we find Jesus experiencing a range of emotions from compassion to anger and grief. He entered the synagogue and found the man with the withered hand. The leaders of the synagogue watched Him to see whether He would heal this man on the Sabbath, which was against Jewish law. His compassion prompted Him to say to the crippled man, "Come here," and He asked His critics, "Is it lawful on the Sabbath to do good or to do harm, to save life or to kill?" They were silent and, we are told, He looked around at them with anger, grieved at their hardness of heart. Their indifference to human suffering and their devious attempt to trap Jesus made Him angry! Gandhi, revered almost to sainthood in this century, was a peaceful, contemplative Indian holy man who claimed that he learned his nonviolent stance from Jesus' model. But while Gandhi, supposedly, never got angry, Jesus certainly did.

I hope you, as a Christian, feel anger. I hope you feel like taking a whip to those people who proliferate our nuclear arms race in our land and other lands. I hope you are angry at indiscriminate abortion. I hope you are angry about rampant pornography, not just in slick magazines but the pornography every one of our television networks pumps out part of the time. I hope you are angry about child abuse. People who are your neighbors and mine are using and abusing children. I hope you are really angry at the recalcitrant racism, which we euphemistically call apartheid in South Africa. Almost nightly, we see the white faces of that nation's leaders on TV, claiming they are not going to budge. They must budge eventually, but, undoubtedly, at the cost of many lives. I hope you are angry at government-sponsored genocide in Ethiopia. The food that compassionate people have sent from around the world rots, because the government doesn't want its opponents to survive. I hope that makes you angry, really angry. It is appropriate to feel anger about all of these things. It is justified.

Jesus experienced anger, and we ought to feel more of it about the evil and corruption around us. But we also know that Jesus wept. He went to the home of His friends, Mary and Martha, after the death of their brother, Lazarus, and He wept. We ought to be free to weep and mourn when somebody we love dies. Even if we're certain they are now in God's presence, we are still lonely and diminished by their loss. You are less because a friend or family member has gone. It's appropriate to weep.

At the end of Matthew's Gospel, we read that Jesus was sorrowful and troubled. He had tried to prepare His disciples for what lay ahead: the arrest, the trial, His inevitable death. He was sorrowful, frightened, and anxious. We know about those feelings because He shared them with His friends. Think of the utter loneliness He experienced on the cross. With His life ebbing, He cried, "My God, my God, why hast Thou forsaken me?" That heartrending cry expressed His feelings of total abandonment.

One of my favorite Bible verses is from John's Gospel, "I came that ye might have joy" (*see* John 15:11). It means so much to me, I have written it on the flyleaf of the Bibles I gave my three children last Christmas. John the Baptist certainly never intimated that he came for that reason. He came to make people feel guilty about their sins. He challenged them to shape up. But, our Lord came, on the heels of John's ministry, with that bold statement, "I came that you might have joy."

Certainly feelings have an important place in all our lives. Feelings can prompt noble actions. Feelings make us alive and fully human. That's what conversion is all about. We are not supposed to turn into spooks. God has all the angels He needs. He wants sons and daughters, fully human, in whom He lives.

John Ruskin has said, "The ennobling difference between one man and another is that one feels more than another." And David Viscott says, "Not to be aware of one's feelings, not to understand them or know them, or use or express them, is worse than being blind, deaf or paralyzed. Not to feel is not to be alive. More than anything else, feelings make us human. Feelings make us all kindred." Your feelings link you up with all the rest of the human race, be they Maasai warriors, Mongolian tribesmen, Nicaraguans, or Russians. We all feel, and that gives us a common bond beyond color and culture. To cease to feel is to be emotionally comatose, cut off from the rest of humanity.

There are couples who spend their whole married life bickering, sometimes for fifty years or more. That seems sad, but I'm convinced that it's better than being bland. There's something better in relationships than being pleasant and polite. God didn't redeem us to make us nice people. The trouble with thinking you must have only good feelings is that you have to deny the bad ones. "I must not be an angry person." Or, "I must not admit I have sexual temptations." When you're determined to have no bad feelings, you put a lid on the good ones. You can't discriminate. When you close that valve off, you end up a very controlled person, unable to express the positive emotions, such as love and joy. The price of being someone who can hug and affirm or love and cry and laugh is that you're also open to those not-so-nice feelings.

Paul writes in his letter to the Ephesians, "Be angry but do not sin; do not let the sun go down on your anger, and give no opportunity to the devil" (4:26, 27 RSV). He says we are not to nurse our anger. Get your anger over with, clear the deck before sundown. If you bottle that feeling up, insisting, "I'm not angry, dear," in a tone which belies that statement, you are giving the forces of evil an opportunity to undermine your faith and witness.

In your personal faith journey I urge you to make your feelings work for you. First of all, enjoy them. They are a gift from God. Don't feel guilty about the negative ones. They're all part and parcel of something you have no control over. One of my friends is a clerk in one of our downtown stores. He tells about a phone call, received in his department over the Christmas holidays. The caller asked about some cardigan sweaters on sale. "Do you have a large in blue?" he asked. "Yes, we do," was the answer. "To what address can we mail it?" "Don't mail it," was the reply. "Bring it to the phone booth in front of the store. I can't get near the counter." Most of us have been in a situation where we can't get the clerk's attention. If you're like me, that makes you angry. This man found a creative way to express his anger and beat the system.

We can make our feelings work for us when we stop fighting the negative ones. Let them come. That's one of the great lessons of Gestalt psychology, and I think it's a biblical approach. Our fear of pain and our repression of negative thoughts gives them inordinate power over us. Gestalt urges us to go into the pain; experience it and it will disappear. During His Crucifixion, Jesus was offered wine to help dull the pain. He refused it. We are in the age of painkillers, indiscriminately used—Valium, tranquilizers, alcohol. These substances are not painkillers. They are killers. The American people are being destroyed by painkillers. If we could go into that pain without tranquilizers, without getting drunk or smoking dope, we might conquer it.

In dealing with feelings, we need above all to "walk in the light," as the beloved disciple, John, wrote in his first letter. The best way to allow God to deal with negative feelings that may prompt you to destructive actions is to have some group, some place where you can confess them. "I'm in trouble. I have sexual temptations. I'm angry at my boss." If you hate your boss for good reasons, maybe the best course is not to confront him or her with your feelings. To begin with, you may want to go to your Christian friends and let some of the anger out.

When I came to my present parish some years ago, I told our staff pastors that anyone dealing with needy and lonely people is in a very vulnerable position. Counseling can all too easily degenerate into some kind of romantic liaison. When that kind of temptation appears, cold showers and prayers are not the answer. I advise them to let somebody know about the problem and to walk in the light and to let God deal with that temptation.

Our feelings can lead us into positive action. Lee Iacocca has become somewhat of a folk hero in our time. He has turned Chrysler Motor Company around and saved jobs for the employees. His best-selling book gives us a clue to his secret of leadership. He lets his feelings work for him. He goes into a new business and he gets angry when things don't go well. He praises and affirms when they do go well. He is not a bland, neutral executive. He communicates his feelings, and people respond.

We need more and more to use our feelings creatively, even our feelings of anger. Sir Thomas Beecham was head of the London Philharmonic for many years. For a time he lived in a flat next door to a lady who played her radio so loudly that he couldn't concentrate on his musical score. He spoke to her often about it, but to no avail. He began to get really angry about the situation. One day he hit upon a solution. He decided to invite the brass section of his orchestra to his flat for a rehearsal. For an hour and a half the brass section of the London Philharmonic played full tilt in that cramped space. His neighbor got the message. He never heard her radio again.

Yes, Christians can get angry. It's okay to curse that fig tree once in a while. When others are being hurt, you should and must get angry. You may need to take whips and drive evildoers out of the temple. When you're being used and abused, it's okay to be angry. It's okay to weep. It's okay to love. It's okay to laugh. Your feelings are your friends. Use them as gifts of God. They don't need to be roadblocks in the faith journey. They can be lamps that light the road.

CHAPTER ELEVEN

The Road to Bethany

IF YOU'VE BEEN to the Holy Land and traveled the road from Jerusalem to Bethany, you know it is a steep and rocky one. It is today and it surely was in Jesus' time, but it is a road He traveled often. One of the reasons was His friendship with the two sisters, Mary and Martha, and their brother Lazarus, who lived there. He went to their home often, I would imagine, just to take off His sandals, have a meal, laugh a bit, be with friends, play, and rest. Refreshed, He could return to the intensive work of proclaiming the Kingdom, preaching, healing, and confronting the religious and political structures of His day. We see in our Lord's life a rhythm—the healthy rhythms of work, play, rest, and worship. He is a model for the rest of us of what a balanced life ought to be.

One of the saddest stories I know concerns a former neighbor of mine. She lived just three doors away from us. She was a beautiful woman in her mid-thirties with a successful husband and handsome family. She was in perfect physical form, not an ounce of fat, every muscle toned. She seemed to me to be a fitness fanatic. She jogged faithfully every morning for six miles or more. She was the top women's seed in singles in our community's tennis ladder. Yet, on one beautiful Florida morning, this perfect physical specimen climbed to the highest building in the area and threw herself off.

It's the kind of tragedy that makes us ask what life is all about. Certainly, there is nothing wrong with being in shape and working to get there. Christians believe the body is the temple of the Holy Spirit. We are to maintain it and preserve it in good working order for God to use. But, the lesson I learned from my neighbor's tragic suicide is that often, when circumstances of our lives become unmanageable, we get lopsided. We tend to make one facet of our life a single consuming passion.

You know people like that. There are the exercise buffs who live for the gym and the track and the handball game. Or, some of us, when life becomes unmanageable, become workaholics. Our job demands all our waking hours, and all other commitments are ignored. We work ten, twelve, fourteen hours a day and, ironically enough, with that kind of dedication we often succeed. We may also lose touch with our families or die young of a coronary attack.

There are any number of ways in which our lives can become lopsided. The opposite of the workaholic is, I suppose, the cool cat—laid back, never ruffled, never involved, no causes. That, to me, is almost more tragic. Perhaps the religious fanatic is the worst—the person who is into the "Word" and absorbed with all things religious. Every time you meet him, he spews out all his experiences. You are simply someone who must be indoctrinated into the same set of beliefs.

The beginning verses of Genesis give us some interesting insights into this whole matter of balance. We read that God made the world in six days and, on the seventh, He rested. God is not Hal, the computer. God is not a microchip. God is not an impersonal force. Machines never have to rest.

They just keep running. But God, who is infinite and perfect, is a personality like you and me and the record indicates that God needed a time to rest—a change of pace if you will. We who are made in His image are created to operate in the same way.

Matthew's Gospel touches on this in the eighth chapter. Jesus went to Peter's house and found his mother-in-law lying sick with a fever. We read that He touched her hand and the fever left her and she rose and served Him. Apparently word of that healing got out, because that evening they brought to Him all sorts of people who were possessed by demons, and He cast out the evil spirits with a word and healed all the sick. It seems only natural that when a healer hits town who doesn't charge and who can cure any and all medical problems, anybody with any health problems at all will seek him out. They'd be stupid not to. Nevertheless, when Jesus saw the great crowds all around Him, clamoring for healing, He gave orders to go over to the other side of the lake. His agenda was not dictated by the sea of human need all around Him. He healed, He left. He worked, He rested.

I am particularly fond of those beautiful verses from the third chapter of Ecclesiastes which remind us that for everything there is a season and a time for every matter under heaven; among those: a time to be born, to die, to kill, to heal, to weep, and to laugh. Verse fifteen seems to sum it all up, "That which is, already has been; that which is to be, already has been; and God seeks what has been driven away" (RSV). In other words, when we're out of balance, God wants us to bring back into our lives those things that have been driven out by obsessions and compulsions.

Four of our basic needs are, obviously, work, play, rest, and worship. Someday I'd like to run a halfway house for people who can't take life's pressures anymore, but still aren't ready for the psychiatric ward. One of my rules would be that for the first three days, one could do nothing but sleep and eat. I'm convinced that 90 percent of our spiritual problems would disappear after three nights of peaceful rest and three days of good nutrition. In the remaining time, we could deal with the other 10 percent of our problems. Then there would be a time for hard work. We'd saw wood, dig ditches, paint buildings. We would play a lot and worship frequently, alone and together. With those four basic needs met, more of us would be open to God's healing.

Saint Theresa of Avila always looked for novices who knew how to laugh, eat, and sleep. She was sure that if they ate heartily they were healthy, if they slept well they were more than likely free of serious sin, and if they laughed, they had the necessary disposition to survive a difficult life.

Arthur Schnabel, that brilliant pianist, was once asked, "What is the secret of your genius at the piano? Is it the way you touch the keys?" "No," he said. "Many pianists touch the keys the way I do. It's the pauses between the touch that make for genius." In the same way, it's the rest between activities that make the activities optimum.

God meant us to be active and passive, playing and worshipping, busy and resting—in both our physical and spiritual lives. That's the ebb and flow described so beautifully in Ecclesiastes.

The pressures of life tend to rob us of this important rhythm. We have external pressure. There's simply too much to do. And if we have any wisdom at all, we're aware that there is simply too much to do for the neighborhood, the job, the church, the world. How do we survive too many opportunities? Earl Wilson, the columnist, once said, "A vacation is what you take when you can no longer take what you've been taking." It seems to me we tend to handle our pressures in at least these three ways:

1. We can try to do everything and attempt to meet all needs. When we do that, we play God. We're headed for certain burnout.
2. We can say, "There's so much to do I can't do anything. I think I'll just go to bed and take a nap."
3. We can wear ourselves out trying to decide what to do and in what order. We can spend our whole life just trying to make decisions.

Two young women from our church, Susan and Nancy, went to Abudabi to work in a hospital. Their chores were many—treating patients, washing newborn babies, reaching out. The work was hard and the hours long. But in one of their letters they shared the reason why they were able to continue there so joyously. They understood that there is enough time in every day to do God's will for you that day. There's not enough time to do all the things you can do, or all the things that need doing. But God is not a hard taskmaster. It's not possible to go to bed saying, "Lord, we did it all," for there will always be a vast sea of unmet needs. But we can do the things that were possible to do today.

On the other hand, you may have decided you will not be the victim of external pressures. You will be inner-directed, self-motivated. That can be a trap for some of us. The internal pressures to excel can be as deadly as the external ones.

Many years ago, I served a small parish in Illinois. I stayed there three years and left feeling somewhat resentful that the congregation demanded so much of me. I realized later that nobody ever required all that activity from me. The pressure was my own.

Transactional Analysis describes a tape inside us that always answers the question, "How am I doing?" with, "Try harder." The answering voice usually sounds like our mother or father or some other primary figure from the past.

Enough is never enough and we do more and more and yet this person inside is never pleased. Those internal pressures backfire, and we end up hating the very people we are supposed to love and serve.

We said that worship is one of our basic needs. The Bible reminds us that man is not made for the Sabbath. The Sabbath is made for man. We go to church for corporate worship so that God may give us Himself and "Shalom," the wholeness and completeness and balance that is so essential. We go out again into the world not as perfect people, but as those living our lives in balance.

Granger Westberg, a Lutheran pastor and pioneer in wholistic health, travels about the country speaking on wellness. When he comes to a new town he often asks, "Where are the health centers?" People invariably mention the hospitals. "No, no," he protests, "those are the sickness centers. That's where you go when you're not well. Where are the places that keep people healthy and whole? The church, the family, the school, all ought to be our wellness centers."

As a church family, we have a rhythm of life, one that should be contributing to our wellness and wholeness throughout the liturgical year. That year follows the life of our Lord and it starts in the fall with Advent. Advent is a time of hope and expectations. It's a time when we sing, "Come Thou Long Expected Jesus." How much we need a season of hope in your life and mine, an expectation that God is going to act, and that tomorrow will be better than today. Advent reminds us of that gift of hope.

At Christmas, we celebrate Christ's birth. It is a time of beginnings. It is an opportunity to think about new beginnings in our lives. What can we start that we haven't done before that involves trusting God? Christmas is, of course, followed by Epiphany. We commemorate the journeys of the Magi. We Christians are pilgrims on a journey. We are not just sitting around waiting for the second coming. We are God's family going somewhere together. In February, Lent begins, and that is a time of sacrifice and increased spiritual discipline, as we remember our Lord's suffering. It is a time to find God's gift in suffering. We ought never to seek suffering, but we need not fear it. God has something good to give, even in the worst of times. Suffering has a purpose, and we need to learn the meaning of it. At Easter we celebrate the Resurrection. The Resurrection symbolizes deliverance. A friend of mine is subject to deep depression. I have prayed for him, but I can't lift his deep depression, and his psychiatrist can't. But, if we believe in the Resurrection, then as the sun burns off the fog, even a depression will eventually leave, and God's sunshine will surround us again. It seems we can only experience the Resurrection in the most desperate of circumstances.

The liturgical year ends with Pentecost. God's Spirit descends and the believers are sent out. Pentecost is the time of claiming God's power and for embarking on mission. Mission, or servanthood, is an important part of the whole rhythm of life.

As you worship throughout the liturgical year, you may need to correct the balance of your life in any one of these areas—by receiving the gift of hope or making a new beginning, by starting a journey, dealing with suffering, by experiencing the Resurrection, or embarking on mission.

Jesus practiced the rhythm of life. The Road to Bethany symbolizes the rest and relaxation part of His earthly life. It is just one part, but it is just possibly the part that made all the other parts possible. When God demanded the ultimate sacrifice, He was ready.

I heard a remarkable story recently about Tommy Lasorda, one of the great baseball managers of our time. He seems to understand that excellence is 99 percent spiritual—

it comes from attitude and motivation. Superior skills do not always make a winning team. He was once asked how he trained players to respond in tense situations—this one for example: It's the bottom half of the ninth inning. The team is ahead three to two; the bases are loaded. A slugger from the opposing team comes up to bat. Now, if you're in center field, or left field, or right field, the normal thing is to be thinking, *O Lord, if the ball comes to me, don't let me drop it. If I miss this one and they win, I'm in disgrace. Don't let the ball come this way.* "Now," he was asked, "how can you prepare your players to deal with those situations?" Tommy said, "That's easy. I prepare them so that when that time comes they'll be saying, 'Hit the ball to me.' "

Those are the two choices we all have. We can live our whole life praying, "O Lord, don't let me fail," or we can live our lives in such balance that when the big moment comes, we're saying, "Lord, hit the ball to me."

CHAPTER TWELVE

Detours on the Road of Faith

I SEEM TO BE fascinated by the frightening. For example, I have an instinctive fear of snakes. If I'm walking down the trail in the woods and suddenly catch sight of one, I have to fight an unreasonable sense of terror. In my mind I know that snakes aren't all that harmful. Even the poisonous ones are not likely to hurt you if you leave them alone. But that logic has not helped me conquer my aversion to snakes. Why is it, then, that my favorite place to visit at the zoo is the reptile house? Safely contained, I never tire of watching snakes and their cousins, the alligators and crocodiles.

I suffer, too, from an illogical fear of heights. I'm not afraid to fly or climb mountains. But when I go up to the top of a skyscraper and walk out on the observation platform and look down, I am suddenly terrified. I'm safe and am certainly not going to jump, but I suffer a little vertigo just looking down from there. That's why it's hard to explain my desire to try, before I get too much older, both parachute jumping and hang gliding.

All of this may explain my fascination over the years with the person of Demas, the man Paul mentions in his letter to Timothy. The only reference is this cryptic one, "But Demas, in love with this present world, has deserted me." Demas is mentioned in just two other places in the New Testament. Paul writes, in Colossians, "Luke and Demas send their love to you."

Demas, we conclude, was a trusted friend and traveling companion and brother in the faith. I think I am intrigued with Demas because of my fear of being like him some day. He, who was once a part of this ragtag band of evangelists and missionaries, braving the dangers and proclaiming the Word, left the fold. He was in the center of the Kingdom, friend of the apostles, and somehow he slipped out of the net. The idea scares me. I think, "Is there no safe place? Will I be next?" The worst fate I can think of is something much worse than snakebite or falling off a building. It is to be a Demas. He who knew Truth loved other things more and fell away.

There's a scene in *The Caine Mutiny,* that wonderful book that's been both a stage play and movie, where Willie, one of the crew members on the minesweeper *Caine,* receives a letter of advice from his dying father: "By the time you get this letter I will be dead. First, there is nothing more precious than time. Wasted hours destroy your life just as surely at the beginning as at the end. Second, religion. I'm afraid I haven't given you much, not having much ourselves. But I think after all I will mail you a Bible before I go into the hospital. Get familiar with the words. You will never regret it. I came to the Bible as I came to everything in life, too late. Third, Willie, think of me as I might have been, at the times in your life when you come to crossroads. And for my sake, and for the sake of a father who often took the wrong turns, take the right ones. Be a man, son. Love, Dad."

Willie is to think of his father as the man he might have been. We can imagine Demas in the ensuing years feeling wistful about that as well. Spiritual failure, it seems to me, is the ultimate tragedy in life, and there are at least two kinds. You can fail first of all by losing your faith. Jesus told the parable of the seeds and it so accurately describes what has happened in the lives of people we know, or perhaps, our own. There are those whose faith blooms so promisingly for a time, but, having no roots, it eventually is scorched or choked by weeds. I went through seminary with two of the most gifted men I've ever known. One was a mass evangelist. He held rallies for thousands and spoke so persuasively of Jesus that hundreds came forward each night to make commitments. This charismatic preacher, in his later years, turned from the faith. He writes novels ridiculing the Resurrection, Jesus, and the faith.

Another friend had a unique ministry to university students. He traveled all over the Ivy League talking to men and women about Christ. He is presently living in a farm community heading up a cult centering on the worship of God in nature. We might well ask, "What happened?" Most of us who have been in the Christian life any length of time can think of at least a few people like that. You think of a friend who stood with you ten, fifteen, twenty years ago through the hard times and the fun times, the tears and the joy. Where is that person now? You have no idea. They are no longer in your church, or in any church. Those lost relationships break your heart.

Central to the good news is the belief that it is never too late to repent and come home. Recently a woman came to see me, and at the beginning of our time together expressed tearfully that she had committed the "unforgivable sin." I said, "Wait a minute. If you had committed the unforgivable sin, you wouldn't be here at all. The unforgivable sin is to insist you haven't sinned and don't need the grace of God. That's the sin against the Holy Spirit. The very fact that you're here in tears and repentant means that you're forgivable." To turn away from the only source of life and hope that we have and refuse the forgiveness Christ offers is the most tragic kind of spiritual failure.

There's another kind, less deadly in its consequences but sad, nevertheless, and that is to come short of the dreams God has for you. If, as believers, we come short of the person that God meant us to be, we are failing spiritually. The great Russian novelist Dostoevski, dead now over one hundred years, is one of history's most powerful examples of this. One of the four or five great novelists of all time, he published his first book at age twenty-five and was a great success. Unable to handle the accompanying fame and riches at such an early age, he began to drink excessively. His rabid anticzarist politics resulted in his arrest, and he was sentenced to die before a firing squad. A pardon arrived just at the moment when the rifles were to be fired. He was, instead, sent off to Siberia for ten years. Once there, he was allowed to have just one book—the New Testament.

For ten years this brilliant young novelist devoured the New Testament and became Christ intoxicated. His greatest books followed on those years: *Crime and Punishment, The Idiot,* and the greatest of all, *The Brothers Karamazov,* all works that profoundly examine the depths of the human soul and the grace of God. But in his new faith, he was totally undisciplined. He didn't belong to a church congregation, he stopped reading his Bible, and ceased to pray. In time he again took to drink. After the death of his wife, he got involved with many women and ended as a broken, wasted, penniless man. We can't help but wonder what he could have been, had he been everything God meant him to be.

A journalist once asked George Bernard Shaw this interesting question: "Mr. Shaw, you have wined and dined with all of the greats of our generation. They all aspire to your

friendship and you know them well. If you could be rein-
carnated and come back as some other famous person of our
time, who would it be?" This is Shaw's response, verbatim:
"If I could relive my life in the role of any person I desired, I
would want to be the man George Bernard Shaw could have
been but wasn't." The man who might have been. Robert
Louis Stevenson put it this way, "To be what we are and to
become what we are capable of becoming is the only end of
life."

There are all sorts of reasons for the kind of spiritual failure we have been talking about. Paul says of Demas that he
deserted the cause because he was in love with this present
world. We could do a good deal of speculating on just what
that means. What kind of bribe, what worldly reward can
the devil dangle to tempt you out of the Kingdom? As for
me, I think I'm vulnerable in at least three major areas; and
perhaps most of us are. First, there is sexual temptation. It
begins as we start to covet somebody who doesn't belong to
us, and if we continue to dwell on those fantasies to the
point where we are making plans to carry them out, we are
entering into an alliance with the powers of darkness, which
endangers our very soul.

Then, of course, there is money. The New Testament is
usually misquoted to read, "Money is the root of all evil." It
is the love of money that is the root of all evil. The love of
money tempts us to cheat in small or large ways, from pad-
ding expense accounts to reneging on debts or actually em-
bezzling money. It is the love of money that makes us
manipulate people to acquire things.

I've always found the New Testament story of the rich
young ruler so affecting. In Mark's account we find Jesus on
the road again, but in His home territory, the area of Judea
beyond the Jordan. He is approached by a young man so
eager to see Him that he is running. He falls at Jesus' feet

and asks life's crucial question: What must I do to inherit eternal life? When he claims to have kept all God's commandments faithfully since boyhood, Mark gives us Jesus' reaction in one moving sentence. "Jesus looking upon him loved him" (Mark 10:21 RSV). He is asked to join the disciples on the journey, but there is one requirement. He is to sell all his possessions and give the money to the poor.

The story does not end happily. We read that "His countenance fell, and he went away sorrowful; for he had great possessions" (Mark 10:22 RSV). This exemplary young man missed God's best plan in order to keep his money. He, like Demas, was in love with this present world, the world of money, privilege, possessions, and power. If renouncing them was the price of eternal life, it was too costly for this promising young man.

But the third common area of temptation is perhaps most insidious—ego. I want honor. I want to be admired. I want to be known. I want credit. I want power. Someone has wisely said that there is no limit to the amount of good you can do, if you don't care who gets the credit.

Demas's defection from the Kingdom might have been the result of succumbing to temptation in any of these areas or, of course, something else entirely. But we are simply told he was "in love with the world."

The world can offer endless pleasures and rewards. The president of McDonald's hamburger chain was quoted as saying, "The three priorities in my life are God, my family, and McDonald's hamburgers. But, when I go to the office, I reverse the order." This might be called the Demas Syndrome. It is so easy to get so caught up in the competition of the marketplace that hamburgers become more important than family or God Himself.

Sometimes we fail to be what God had in mind when He thought of us, because we are trying so hard to be what others want us to be, to live our life on someone else's agenda. Jesus had that problem with His family. On one occasion, His mother sent His brothers into a meeting to persuade Him to stop teaching and healing and come back home to the carpenter shop. We miss God's dream for us in trying to be what Mommy and Daddy want, what our husband or wife wants or what our friends or employers want. We miss God's best when we try to be like somebody else, or even like Jesus.

What is this cult in our time of trying to be like Jesus? There is nobody in the New Testament who is like Jesus. Certainly not Paul, but neither is Peter or Luke or Mary or Martha or Lydia or Priscilla like Jesus. Only Jesus is like Jesus. The job is taken. He promises to come in and live His life in us totally, and to make His home in us. His presence makes us totally unique and different from anyone else, just as each snowflake is unlike any other.

We've been talking about spiritual failure, but what about spiritual success? How do we aim for that? Begin by asking God for the right dream for your life personally and vocationally. One of the great English-language dramas is Arthur Miller's play *Death of a Salesman*. It's the story of Willie Loman, a tragic figure who is trying so desperately to be something he was never meant to be, a super, hotshot salesman making all sorts of profitable deals. He fails miserably and at the end of the play he dies. But he was a gifted carpenter and craftsman, and at one point he built a new front porch for the family home. At the end of the play his son says, "There's more of him in that front stoop than in all the sales he ever made. He had the wrong dreams."

It's okay to start off on the wrong dream, groping your way along, but are you interruptible? A man named Tom Rooney worked for Shell Oil some years ago. He was sent to Nigeria, and while driving a company car down a back road, he came upon a little village where a crowd had gathered around a woman in labor. It seemed she had been lying there for two days attempting to give birth. Rooney was horrified. "Put her in my car," he said. The woman was duly stowed into the car with her husband, and they set off to find a doctor or hospital. Unfortunately, the woman died en route. They stopped the car and with Rooney's help, the husband buried her right on the spot, no graveclothes, no casket.

The incident so devastated Rooney that he went back to London and quit his job. He was determined to go back to Africa and be some little part of getting basic hygiene and medical care to people who were dying unnecessarily. He became a Catholic priest and now heads up the World Mercy Fund committed to help and hope for the people of Africa. Just suppose, though, that God wasn't able to interrupt him. He might have said, "I can't give up my pension and tenure with Shell Oil." He might have missed his dream.

Let's remember that even with the right dream, we're not promised an easy life. Easy is not the name of the game. We lived for six years in Florida, which is full of mosquitos, cockroaches, and bugs of all sorts. It's a state that can and does support a great many exterminators. A company in our town was called the "No Risk Exterminators." I suppose that meant that if you still had cockroaches after their treatment, you'd get your money back. There was no risk involved. That's just what a lot of people want in terms of their faith. No-risk faith. But genuine faith requires risk. Jesus says, "Lo, I will be with you always, until the end of the world"—but He also says, "He who would lose his life for my sake, shall find it."

G. Campbell Morgan was one of the great English preachers and a powerful man of God. As a young seminary student he fell in love with a certain young woman. He was reluctant to propose. He said, "I think God has laid it on my heart to say some radical things to the church. I may not be a success, I may be persecuted. I don't want to drag you into that. In five or six years, perhaps I'll be established, and then I can offer you my hand in marriage." Her immediate reply was, "If I can't climb the mountain with you, I'd be ashamed to meet you at the top."

I'm convinced that spiritual success is, above all, a matter of trust. Paul writes to his young friend Timothy, "I have fought the good fight; I've finished the race; I've kept the faith" (*see* 2 Timothy 4:7). Toward the end of the letter he says, "The Lord stood by me and gave me strength to proclaim the word fully, that all the Gentiles might hear it. So I was rescued from the lion's mouth. The Lord will rescue me from every evil and save me for his heavenly kingdom. To him be the glory forever and ever" (2 Timothy 4:17, 18 RSV). Paul is trusting God even though he faces death. He faces old age. He faces persecution. But he knows he is not alone.

We are not all facing persecution, but we are all facing both death and old age, or perhaps middle age. I've been told that Hollywood has come up with an answer to the horror of middle age. They simply call it "Youth—Part II." For some of us, Youth—Part III is coming. But there's nothing ahead that can defeat us as long as we're following God's dreams.

The rich young ruler met Jesus on the road and was invited to continue with Him, but instead took another road of his own choice. We all come to those places. We may choose another route, one which proves to be a dead end, or only a detour. But, if we're following God's dream for our lives, we'll trust in Jesus and go His way. The road may be dusty, hot, rocky, sometimes muddy, as it was for the disciples, but He'll be with us "even to the end of the earth."

CHAPTER THIRTEEN

The Road Home

A MAN I know went to his class reunion a few months ago. I asked him how it went. "It was terrible," he confessed. "My classmates were all so old and fat and bald that none of them recognized me." Sometimes revisiting past scenes is not altogether happy. At best, there is a poignancy in seeing the familiar people and places where we were once so at home.

But I would like you to remember with me right now the first time you were homesick. Can you remember where you were . . . how old you were . . . the home you were separated from . . . the family members you left? I remember vividly the first time I felt estranged and separated from the place where I belonged. I was seven years old. My parents had sent me to a church camp, Camp Gray on the shores of Lake Michigan, for two weeks. And for two weeks I was sick to my stomach. The nights were interminable and I remember lying in my bunk, wondering how I could go home and still save face. If only I could go home. I didn't belong with all those strange people. My only positive memory was that I had my first fight at that camp and won. I triumphed over the son of a McCormick Seminary professor. But the feeling I remember most is one of homesickness. "Would I ever be home again?"

I'm sure you can remember times like that. Homesickness is more than missing a place. Usually we are missing someone who cares for us and is waiting for our return. And if that person or persons is somewhere else, why are we here? Will the time ever come when we can go home again? Somehow that song, "Tie a Yellow Ribbon," captures those feelings again for us. The character in the song is wandering in the far country like the Prodigal Son. He has blown it, done some dumb things, things for which he is ashamed. Finally he writes a letter: "Hey, family, I'd like to come home. If you don't want me back, I can't blame you. But if you do, would you put a yellow ribbon on the old oak tree in the yard? I'll ride by and if there's no ribbon, I'll just keep moving on." Most of us still get choked up when we get to the place where our hero goes by and finds the tree so full of yellow ribbons, he can't see the branches. It may be a little corny, but most of us were so gripped by the idea, that the yellow ribbon became a national symbol a few years ago, affirming our hope in the safe return of the hostages from Iran.

No matter where we've been or what we've done, there's a time to come home. We belong. This is the message at the heart of the gospel. The Good News in Jesus is that there is a homecoming, a gathering for all of us. He has come to make it okay for you and me to come home to the place where we really belong. We don't belong in a far country. We're not at home with some of the foolish things we've done. God is at the center of the gathering, the reunion. He is your real Father, who figuratively ties a million yellow ribbons in the tree and says, "I know. I understand. Yes, you've been dumb. Yes, you've been selfish. Yes, you've been foolish. But come home." Is that news too good to be true? It is at the heart of what you and I believe as Christians.

Perhaps the most poignant story Jesus ever told was the parable of the father with two sons. Those of us who are parents have only to hear the opening line—that a certain man had two sons—and we immediately know there are problems ahead. If you've had two or more children, you are impressed by the miracle of personality. Each child is entirely unique. In the story Jesus tells, one son says to the father, "I want to go out into the world and make my fortune." Now most of us parents know our children pretty well. The father probably knew, within certain limits, what was in his son's heart. The story is astonishing because (and just think of this if you pride yourself on being a godly parent) the father does not just say, "It's okay. You can go." Knowing his child well enough to predict the disaster that will result, the father nevertheless says (to put it in today's vernacular), "Here's a whole fistful of traveler's checks." He pays the bill for this foolhardy adventure.

Love does not control or manipulate. You and I as parents cannot always control the children we love, even for their own good. Wanting the best for our children, we try to protect them from foolish decisions. But God doesn't do that. The father Jesus describes says you're free to come and you're free to go.

This parable teaches us a second thing about the nature of God's love—God is not a rescuer. The father does not send a CARE package to the far country though news of the son's plight probably reached him. You better believe people haven't changed much since those times. Neighbors who journeyed to the far country, as traveling salesmen, or off on a theater tour, or whatever, were eager to come back with the bad news. "Oh, let me tell you about your son. You won't believe what he's doing." Those stories must have grieved the father, but he doesn't write, he doesn't send food or money. The son knows the way home, and the father gives the son the dignity of managing his own life. The son could live there as long as he wanted and though the father is brokenhearted, there are no attempts to rescue the boy.

When we were living in Florida, we were involved with a wonderful Christian family who had an adopted son who had gone to the far country and lived it up in every way—sex, drugs, booze, whatever. They did everything to help him. They went to see him, sent money, shamed him, prayed for him. They finally came to the place where they said, "We can't do anymore." And they didn't. In a matter of months their son came home on his own initiative. He got homesick. He came home healed and the rejoicing was enormous.

The turning point in the parable Jesus told is when the son in the far country comes to himself. Just what does that mean? I heard about an old country parson who preached on that subject. He said, "This young man became so destitute, he sold his coat to buy bread, then he sold his shirt to buy bread. Finally, he sold his underwear for bread and then he came to himself." We'd like to call that experience of "coming to himself" a conviction of sin. But there's no indication that this young man is convicted of anything or sees the error of his wicked ways. What he says is, "How dumb I am to be here starving. My father's hired servants live better than this. I can't go back as a son again but since my father is a compassionate man, I will go back and ask to be one of his servants. I will go home and say to him (because this may make points with the old man), 'Father, I've sinned.'" But his motivation is to better himself. He comes to himself when he assesses his situation. What am I doing here? I don't belong here. I'm out of place. I'm going back where things are better.

Is it possible that you and I can really begin again? I recently heard a pertinent story about George Bernard Shaw, the famous playwright and critic. At age ninety he was very ill and close to death. He was so weak he could speak only with great effort. But at one point he leaned over and said to his nurse, "Dear, would you do me a favor? When the doctor comes in and says that I'm dead, would you ask for a second opinion?" Usually we need a second opinion on our condition, whatever it is. If somebody has said you're dead (or hopeless, which is about the same thing), get a second opinion from God. If you've been told, "You've had it; you've blown it," God wants to give you a second opinion. You can come home again.

I spent a day recently visiting one of the great rescue missions in our town. I toured the building and met many of the men. The director was taking me around, and I was moved to see the compassion that those people have in caring for the lost and the least. Toward the end of my visit, the director made an interesting observation. "You know it's a strange thing. When I ask the older men and women who come here about their problems, they invariably say, 'I'm a failure, that's why I'm here. I've been dumb and foolish and wasted my life.' They have a clear sense of right and wrong, good and evil, and they're ready to deal with their failures. The younger people who come in, those in their teens and twenties, have no sense of right and wrong. They have no insight into the cause of their problems. They tend to blame circumstances, society, their parents. There's no sense of having done anything wrong."

But Jesus' parable implies that you don't necessarily have to have a conviction of sin to come home. You can come home when you realize that you don't need to continue living in harmful ways. God has something better for you. Perhaps it's easier to come home if you are caught in destructive

behavior and want to change. But if you're living a life of responsibility and respectability, it's much harder to confess
that you long to come home.

When I lived in Florida, I had a retired neighbor who was
remarkably active. He served on the City Council; he was a
senior vestryman in his church. One weekend he went off to
a gathering led by lay people where he made a new beginning with God. Later, he was sharing this experience with
me and another neighbor, an avowed atheist. I said, "Dick,
what's happened to you?" "It's hard to describe," he said.
"I'll tell you I found that I'm loved and that Jesus is real. It
was the most exciting weekend of my life." The conversation really puzzled my nonchurched neighbor, and he spoke
to me about it later. "Bruce, I really don't understand what
happened to Dick. He has always been a good man." I
agreed, "Yes, he has. And it must be much harder for a good
man to be aware of his needs and to come home."

Finally, this story of the father and the Prodigal Son
teaches us that love does not make conditions. Love does
not say, "Well, okay, you're back home now. You must
never leave again." A cartoon I saw years ago in *The New
Yorker* caught the infinite dimensions of the unconditional
love God has for us. The drawing was a biblical scene of the
Prodigal Son, the father, the neighbors, all in their white
robes. The father is about to carve a huge roasted calf when
he turns to his son with a worried look and says, "Now, after
all, son, this is the fourth fatted calf."

Can you really believe that the Father will kill four or
forty-four fatted calves for us? Do you really believe that we
can come home again and again? Each time we leave, we
break His heart, and hurt ourselves and others. But there is a
family gathering where we can come home again and again.
The truly tragic figure is the son who never left home or did
an irresponsible thing. He couldn't rejoice and join the

party. He didn't understand and was furious. He says, "I've been here all the time and you never gave me a goat for a party with my friends." Someone suggested that with his niggardly spirit one mutton chop would be enough to serve the whole group.

You see, it's not enough to be in the household of God doing the right thing. When we insist that we have never done anything wrong, we can't come home. In the parable, the father says, "Son, don't you understand? Everything I have is yours." But the son wanted his wages. He wanted exactly what his brother got. The father tried to explain that everything he possessed was his to share, but the elder brother insisted on getting just what was coming to him. He was as lost as his brother had been. In insisting on what was due him, he missed out on the riches the father wanted to give him.

Jesus came to tell us that it's time to come home, whoever we are. That's where the faith journey leads. Come as you are!

CHAPTER FOURTEEN

The Road to the Stable

THE ROAD to the Stable was traveled by at least three different sets of people, according to the gospel writers. In chronological order, the first, of course, were Mary and Joseph. Next, the shepherds. And, finally, the Magi with their gifts. I guess it's hard to separate the celebration of the birth of the Christ Child from the giving of gifts, and perhaps it is that last group that we have to thank for that.

Those three wise men were aware that ultimate truth had come into the world and they came to worship. Worship always involves gifts—or sacrifice. We're told they brought gold, frankincense, and myrrh. Apart from their monetary worth, perhaps these gifts had a symbolic meaning.

Gold represents the substantial, the real stuff of this world. Frankincense is a very precious kind of incense. It's symbolic of the insubstantial, the creative, that which gives life its flavor and aroma. The third gift, myrrh, is a very precious ointment used for embalming. Perhaps that gift symbolized all that endures beyond this transitory world. But on a more practical level, maybe those expensive gifts, gifts fit for a king, were to be used to support Mary and Joseph in their long exile in Egypt. But whatever these first gifts meant, or however they were used, it's hard to separate the first

Christmas from those first three givers and their extravagant presents.

Most of us are involved with gift giving during the Christmas season. I lived in New Jersey for many years, and while I was not in a pastorate, I would invariably be asked to lead a Christmas Eve midnight service in a neighboring town. Each year I would arrive home about 1:30, and my wife and I would start bringing all the gifts out of hiding—things stored away from the inquisitive eyes of three young children. From 1:30 until 3:00 or 4:00, I would try to maintain the Christmas spirit while putting lug nut A into washer B after you had used rod C. The parts were rarely all there and I have never been mechanically inclined. The gifts of Christmas were almost my undoing.

Thinking about the gifts of Christmas past seems to evoke some of my best and some of my most painful memories. My mother was one of those people who dearly loved Christmas. She usually went out and got a part-time job during that season. She wanted to have extra cash to buy gifts for my dad and me, and for my father's family by his first wife, a daughter and her four children. She always managed to provide extravagant gifts for all of us, way beyond what we could ordinarily afford. One Christmas, after all of the gifts were opened and we were alone, I found her crying. She had received only one present, a bread box. I was probably only eight, but I realized for the first time that adults are as vulnerable as children. Even adults can feel neglected and unloved.

I remember my first Christmas as an army private. I wangled leave and spent a marvelous holiday back home in Chicago. That turned out to be my last visit with my father, who died shortly thereafter. The next Christmas I was overseas, a sergeant in the infantry, dug in on the front lines facing German troops. For some strange reason, nobody fired a shot that Christmas. There were no casualties for just that one night. There was a strange, mysterious silence, as if those deadly enemies had agreed to take time out to worship the Christ Child. This peace-by-mutual-consent was short-lived. Just a week later on New Year's Eve, the Battle of the Bulge began, with the accompanying slaughter of many of my friends, as well as countless Germans.

I remember my first Christmas as a married man. I bought my wife her very first cashmere sweater. She was surprised, to say the least. I've thought about that since. I was a seminary student, and she was earning thirty-five dollars a week. We were living on her income, so I really bought that sweater with her money, but she seemed delighted with it anyway.

There is the familiar story by O. Henry called "The Gift of the Magi," in which a struggling pair of young marrieds are trying to buy Christmas gifts for each other. The husband's only treasure is the gold watch his father had given him. Her prize possession is her long, golden hair. He sells his watch to buy her a comb for that lovely hair, only to find out that she has cut and sold it to buy him a chain for his watch. Somehow, Christmas is the time for making sacrifices.

Even the poorest child expects a gift at Christmas, and that's as it should be. Our local newspaper featured a story one holiday season about a little girl named Stacey. Stacey lives in a little town near our city, and she wrote to her grandmother. She begins the letter philosophically. "Grandmother, why is it that rich people have the money and poor people don't?" She goes on to say that she had to give up flute lessons because her parents couldn't afford the ten-dollars-a-month rent for the instrument. Furthermore, the family was being evicted from their trailer. The very next day, gifts flowed in from all over the area. Stacey had a tree in her trailer, and presents under it. Somebody bought her a flute. Cash gifts paid the rent for the next three months. It's not an unusual story. Even the most uncharitable, believers or nonbelievers, want a child's Christmas to be full of good surprises.

God had a gift for the world in that Baby born in the stable at Bethlehem. God came in Jesus to call us to be His friends, to tell us that in His eyes we are of enormous worth. The very hairs of our head are numbered. Jesus reminded us that as God cares even for the sparrows, He cares much more for us. In those times, the sparrow was the cheapest available meat. You could buy one for a penny. If even the sparrows have worth in God's eyes, how much more worthwhile are we. We are as precious to God as if He had made no one else. As it happens, He has a whole world full of children, but, if we were alone in the universe, we would still merit His undivided attention.

There's a story about an old peasant in France who was sitting in the back pew of an empty church one day. The parish priest came by and asked what he was waiting for. "Nothing," said the old man, "I'm looking at Him and He is looking at me." Worship is not only a time to meet and adore the Lord. It's a time when He reciprocates with delight and love. Worship is two-way communication, an exchange of love between the Creator and the created.

In this two-way exchange, let's consider some of the gifts you and I could give back to our Lord out of gratitude for the unspeakable gift of His love and attention. One might be a boldness to speak about Him. Paul writes, "I am not ashamed of the gospel of Christ: for it is the power of God unto salvation ..." (Romans 1:16 KJV). There are those occasions when we are ashamed in public of the people we love and admire in private. I was always a little ashamed of my father. He was old enough to be my grandfather and he had a funny Swedish accent. I loved him dearly, and I was so ashamed of being ashamed. When I had my first serious girl friend and my friends discovered my secret love, I said, "Her? Who likes her?" I was ashamed to be identified with her, even though I loved her madly.

I have been corresponding with a young woman, a clergyman's daughter, who claims she was twenty-three years old before she understood and responded to the gospel. In her most recent letter, she related an interesting story. "The other day I got something in the mail from Jews for Jesus. It made me realize that I had never tried to tell anyone about Jesus. I work in a bank, and my favorite co-worker happens to be Jewish. She is the one person who makes the job bearable for the rest of us. She affirms, she loves, she is kind and generous. I wondered if she had ever really heard about Jesus.

"Yet, who was I to tell her? One evening, when I had invited her to dinner, I made a deal with God. I promised Him, 'I will not say a word about you unless you open the door. I'm not going to push.' During dinner my friend asked what it was like to be a minister's daughter. It was the perfect opening. As it turned out, she was very interested and had done a lot of reading. I was able to tell her about the Jesus I had met at age twenty-three, and she was really intrigued. We have a whole new relationship."

We need to get over feeling, "Who am I to tell anyone about God?" Rather, how can we not talk about the most wonderful Person in the world?

Fruitfulness is another gift that we know is pleasing to Him, which we can all offer to God. Our lives bear fruit when we care, become involved, help, give, go across the street or across the world. Go to your job on Monday morning prepared to be fruitful—to go the second mile with someone. We can do that. You and I are not capable of being perfect people, but we are forgiven people, and we can be fruitful people. We read in the Psalms that "as far as the east is from the west, so far does he remove our transgressions from us (Psalms 103:12 RSV)."

There's a cardinal in the Philippines named Sin. He has the dubious distinction of being a Cardinal Sin. I have heard that back when he was a bishop, there was a young woman in his parish who claimed to see visions of Jesus. Bishop Sin was asked by his superiors to check her out. He called her into his office. "My dear," he said, "I hear that you see and talk to Jesus. Next time you see Him, would you please ask Him what sin your bishop committed when he was a young theologian?" This seemed a reliable test since no one else knew about that particular sin except Jesus and the bishop's confessor. On the next visit, the young woman again claimed she had seen Jesus.

"Did you ask Him about the sin I committed as a young man?"

"Yes, I did."

"What was His reply?" the bishop asked.

"His reply was, 'I don't remember.' "

God has given us that gift in Jesus. Those shameful things that we have done are not only forgiven, they are no longer remembered. Therefore we can move on and be fruitful.

I have mentioned in earlier books how I was converted while in the army overseas. Back home again, celebrating my first Christmas as a new Christian, I wanted to spiritualize the holiday entirely. I resented the secular trappings, especially the presents. I now see the fallacy of that. Christmas and gifts are inseparable. They have been since the Magi traveled the road to the stable to visit the Christ Child. That Child was God incarnate, the ultimate revelation of His love, which transcended all previous revelations. Through the patriarchs, prophets, and kings, God had tried to communicate His love to us through the ages. The incarnation was and is His last hope.

There's a wonderful story about a farmer who opted to stay at home while his wife and children went off on Christmas Eve to a candlelight service. He himself was an unbeliever and considered the Christmas story nonsense and at best a harmless myth. Nevertheless, he sent the family off cheerfully, content to spend the evening alone. It happened to be a cold, windy night with light snow falling. Going to the window, he spied a flock of birds who seemed to be suffering in the extreme weather, some literally dropping dead.

Anxious to help them, he went out to open the barn door and to get a smudge fire going for warmth. But the birds seemed unaware of this refuge, and wouldn't go into the barn. Next, he tried, with a blanket, to shoo the flock in. Still they scattered. He could think of no way to tell them how to find safety and survival. In his frustration, it occurred to him, "If only I was a bird, I could tell them. . . ." Suddenly the impact of the thought rocked him. That was the crux of the Christmas message. With a sense of wonder, he rushed back to the house, bundled up in his coat and drove off to town to join the family at church.

He understood the incarnation for the first time. To communicate with us, God became one of us. He became one of us to redeem us, to take upon Himself our frailties and burdens. He became one of us to die for our sins. That's the message we find at the end of the Road to the Stable.

CHAPTER FIFTEEN

The Last Road

ONE OF THE last roads Jesus traveled in His peripatetic ministry all over Palestine was the one from Bethany to Jerusalem on that original Palm Sunday. It was the beginning of a nightmare week of confusing events. Rival political groups came together in an evil conspiracy to murder their common enemy. Pilate, the Roman governor of the land, was in an agony of indecision about whether to act with integrity or expediency. Meanwhile, his wife was wracked with horrible dreams. Peter the Rock crumbled and folded and turned into Peter the Wimp at a young girl's questions. A mother's heart was forever broken. The treasurer of the twelve disciples hung himself. An earthquake shook the city. A convicted thief entered Paradise. A secret believer, a member of the Sanhedrin, came out of the closet to claim the dead body for burial.

That fateful Palm Sunday parade followed the route from Bethany down the Kidron Valley and up again to the city. On a recent pilgrimage to the Holy Land with some parishioners, a group of us decided to take that walk, a distance of three to five miles down stony pathways. We went by car to Bethany and started the journey that Jesus Himself must have taken, not just on that first Palm Sunday, but many times. As we followed the route of that first triumphal entry, there was singing and silence, there was laughter and prayer. Halfway through the walk, we arrived at Bethpage, the place where Jesus found the donkey waiting for Him. There is a church there now that is purportedly over the very stone Jesus stood on to climb onto the donkey. It is guarded by a peg-legged gatekeeper who has served there for twenty years that I know of. If you tell him how happy you are to be there, and express that tangibly, which we did, you are invited in to see the church. We stood inside and sang hymns and felt an extraordinary sense of the presence of the Holy Spirit.

Later, we continued down to the Mount of Olives and into the valley before the road went upward once more and we found ourselves on a goat path to the gate through which Jesus rode, while the multitudes cheered. The gate has been bricked up for many years, and the Jewish tradition is that the Messiah will some day come through that gate. Doesn't that say it all about our human perverseness? They are waiting for their deliverer to come through a bricked-up gate. To further complicate the matter, when the Muslims occupied the land years ago, they used the area right outside the gate for a cemetery, just to ensure that no Messiah would come via that route. He could not and would not cross a defiled area. The irony in all of this is, of course, that the Messiah has already come through that very gate.

It's with a strange feeling of sadness that we recall that first Palm Sunday. That triumphal procession somehow spelled out the whole drama of redemption. God from His end was working to change our life and destiny. But, from the human perspective, Palm Sunday is a sad commentary on the human condition, the reluctance we feel about receiving what God wants so much to give us.

Imagine for a moment that a television crew was there to film this drama. There would probably be three or more cameras. One crew would be covering the crowd. What does the man in the street have to say about this parade? We can imagine the reporter asking, "What do you make of this triumphal entry?" There would be a variety of answers, but the consensus might be something like this: "Poor Jesus, that Nazarene prophet! He has tried everything—preaching, teaching, healing, miracles—and they still don't listen and they won't change. What has He got to lose? This may be His last hurrah."

From the point of view of the person on the street, this parade represents a mixture of hope, desperation, and courage. *The Last Hurrah* is the name of a book and a movie about a burned-out, used-up, somewhat shady Boston politician who attempts a comeback one more time. His last hurrah is a pathetic attempt to win the allegiance of voters and be restored to former glory. That kind of last hurrah is something a lot of us have attempted. Steve McQueen, in the last months of his life, was riddled with cancer. A trip to Mexico was his last hurrah, one desperate chance to find a cancer cure not available in the States. He had nothing to lose.

A faltering marriage can be the setting for a last hurrah. Two people who have made a mess of their relationship through betrayal, broken promises, or just lack of communication, can come to the place where they are willing to give it one more chance. "What have we got to lose?" Barney Clark's trip to Salt Lake City was a last hurrah. Facing death anyway, why not have the doctors try an artificial heart implant? This was the last desperate effort for that brave man from Seattle.

I have a dear old friend who is presently staging her last hurrah. She is one of God's most effective servants, who has been the instrument for the conversion and healing of countless people. But she is losing her sight. Everything possible has been done medically and spiritually, but her sight is almost gone. She is facing a frightening future with rare courage. Courage is the stuff of a last hurrah. Edna St. Vincent Millay wrote about similar courage in a moving poem about her mother.

> The courage that my mother had went with her
>   and is with her still.
> Rock from New England quarried,
>   now granite in a granite hill.
> The golden brooch my mother wore
>   she left behind for me to wear.
> I have no thing I treasure more,
>   yet it is something I could spare.
> Oh, if instead, she had left to me
>   the thing she took into the grave.
> That courage like a rock which she has no more need of
>   and I have.

On that first Palm Sunday, the man in the street might have assessed the events from that human perspective, that it was one last try. With courage born of desperation, Jesus was staging a royal parade that might at last make His identity clear.

Meanwhile, let's pick up the second camera crew, photographing the principal actor, Jesus Himself. What about the Palm Sunday events from His point of view? Perhaps Hebrews 4:15 explains it. "For we have not a high priest who is unable to sympathize with our weaknesses, but one who in every respect has been tempted as we are, yet without sinning" (RSV). When God became man in Jesus, He became totally man. It seems likely that that first Palm Sunday looked about the same to Him as it did to the man in the street. It really was His last hurrah. Being totally human, He did not have that divine perspective to see ahead to the events of the week and the ultimate triumph on the cross. The wonder of it! God making one last, desperate attempt to reach us to try to make us understand who He is.

Those Palm Sunday events fulfilled the Old Testament prophecy that a king would come seated on an ass, but I don't think that was the primary motive for Jesus' actions on that day. En route, He wept over Jerusalem, desolate that hearts continued to be hardened to His message. I think the parade was a calculated attempt to give them one last chance.

Sören Kierkegaard writes: "My complaint is not that this age is wicked, but that it is paltry. It lacks passion." Sydney Harris, the columnist, writes: "Movements are so often taken away from their conceivers and captured by fanatics because ordinary persons lack the single-mindedness that characterizes the zealot. A balanced personality will not devote all its energy to a single cause and so leadership passes by default to the energetic extremist." Jesus was the ultimate passionate leader. Would that we could be as single-minded and passionate in His cause. Our lack of zeal creates that vacuum Harris is talking about, and the crazy radicals are left to carry the day.

Assuming this parade represents Jesus' last hurrah, what was the purpose of it? I think it is consistent with His purpose in all the other events of the gospels. He is proclaiming a Kingdom of which He is the King. Perhaps the last hurrah is for His disciples as much as for Himself. He knew they had bet everything on His Messiahship. If only for their sakes, He wanted to try one last time to establish His Kingdom. He was giving all those frightened followers one last chance to respond—the sick, the weak, the outcast, the lost, those who were standing in the shadows, only dimly understanding what was happening, and without the courage to be numbered among the faithful. That parade would give them a chance to stop wavering and come out and be counted.

Recently I received a postcard with no return address, signed simply, "Terry." It said: "Mr. Larson: I am writing to thank you for your sermon. Just when I think I'm going to hang it all up, the Lord puts people and events in my life that give me the slap in the face that I need to get my life back into perspective. . . . This past year has not been as wonderful as I had been planning it to be. These days I am still in school, but spend a lot of time on the Avenue [the University district's main street] with my friends. I am one of those obnoxious characters riding a skateboard, whose aim in life, many think, is to run down old ladies with canes. I do live at home, and my folks are being rather calm about my temporary rebel lifestyle, and we get along rather bully. I try to listen to your messages every week on the radio and hope to come some morning [but] I need someone to come with me for moral support." I couldn't help but think that there must be a lot of Terrys out there, just as there were on that first Palm Sunday, men and women in the shadows, listening and watching, intrigued by the King and His Kingdom, but without the courage to do anything about it.

At Gethsemane, Jesus said, "O Lord, may this cup pass from me." On the cross, He cried, "My God, why hast thou forsaken me?" As far as we know, Jesus had no knowledge of His final victory as the Messiah. In that, He is like Abraham who died without seeing that great nation promised to him. Moses never entered the Promised Land. David was not allowed to build the temple he dreamed of. There are present-day saints, as well, whose victory came only after death. Nate Saint was one of those five missionaries killed by the Aucas in South America. Art Beals, former president of World Concern, and now mission pastor of our Seattle church, became a missionary himself because of the death of those five men. He visited the widow of Nate Saint some time ago in her home, and in the course of conversation, he found himself glancing at the stair landing where a spear was prominently displayed. He asked her about it. "I thought you'd ask about that," she said. "That's the spear that killed my husband. Do you know that the man who threw that spear baptized our son? He has become a Christian pastor." Nate Saint couldn't have known that would happen. He died uncertain of any victory.

But let's pick up the third camera crew. This crew is going to report Palm Sunday from God's perspective. From His perspective, Palm Sunday is not the last hurrah. It is the first. It is the prelude to victory. There is a Salvadore Dali painting in the art museum in Glasgow entitled *Christ of St. John of the Cross* and it is a controversial one. The Crucifixion is depicted from God's perspective. The cross is viewed from above and you see the central beams, our Lord's head and arms, and down below, the world, all of us strange, perverse, and wonderful creatures. A small shaft of light beams from the cross, illuminating the world, but above that cross is a dark, ominous, and omnipresent cloud. The cross seems to be holding back the blackness and allowing the light to penetrate the world. It's one artist's graphic picture of the message of the atonement. Those dramatic events of that first Holy Week represent the first hurrah from God's point of view, in your life and mine.

Ralph Sockman, one of this century's most effective preachers, said, "The cross isn't the price that man had to pay to break God's heart. The cross is the price that God had to pay to break man's heart." Fulton Sheen has said that half the world wants a Christ without a cross, a bland

and moral teacher. And many churches proclaim that Christ. The other half, according to Sheen, wants a cross without a Christ. We want a cross that can be used to lay burdens on the faithful, that they might shape up and stay in line.

That first cross was hideous and frightening. But where is the cross to be found now? It looms over cities from the steeple of downtown churches. It hangs around the neck of a fourteen-year-old street kid who is selling her body. It is a piece of jewelry on an overfed matron who rarely goes to church. It surrounds the Kremlin from churches all over Red Square. The cross is now back in the classrooms of Poland. The cross, symbol of God's grace and man's redemption, is everywhere.

Where does this battle for your soul and mine and for the world take place? The Zealots of Jesus' time thought it took place on a battlefield. They felt they must organize resistance to Roman rule and free their land and its people. Masada was the last hurrah for that group. It was on that high and desolate plain over the Dead Sea where they made their last stand and, in the end, committed mass suicide, every man, woman, and child, in order to thwart their Roman foes.

The Essenes had a different solution, and we might say that the Qumran community where the Dead Sea scrolls were found represents their last hurrah. They sought salvation through withdrawal, by going off into the desert to pray and study.

Unlike the Essenes or the Zealots, Jesus staged the battle over the souls of men and women in a very different theater. He took the battle right down to the street. That Palm Sunday parade route went right through the center of Jerusalem, and it still passes right by where you and I live out our lives. He comes by now, as He did then, giving us an opportunity to cheer and join the parade.

You may be at the point in your journey when a last hurrah is the only course possible. Remember that while it seems, from your point of view, your last hurrah, it may be God's first hurrah.

CHAPTER SIXTEEN

The Road to the Empty Tomb

W<small>E CAN ONLY</small> imagine the anguish those women, Mary and Mary Magdalene, were experiencing as they made their way to Jesus' tomb that first Easter morning. At the tomb, however, according to Matthew's Gospel, they were confronted by an angel with the greeting, "He has risen. Go and tell His disciples." We are told that with fear and great joy, they ran to tell the news to those men who had traveled with our Lord, knew Him best, and loved Him deepest. Their response? "It's an idle tale."

It seems to me that's a sensible reaction. No matter how much you love someone, the Resurrection seems, at first, an idle tale. Someone has described the Easter story using the analogy of a baseball game. At the bottom half of the ninth inning, with your team behind 20–0, you decide to go home and avoid the rush in the parking lot. However, in the next day's newspaper you find that somehow your team won. I'd extend that analogy a little. Let's say you *stayed* 'til the end of the game with a 20–0 final score and then read in the paper the following morning that your team actually won. It would not make any sense. No wonder the disciples had a hard time with the logic of the Easter message.

143

Believing the unbelievable requires faith. It is only by
faith that we Christians believe in the whole incarnation
story—that God, in the person of Jesus Christ, has entered
human history. Some of us have great difficulty coming to
that place.

One of the psychiatrists in our parish, in observing patients over a number of years, has concluded, "Some people
seem to have inherited great faith genes. They're born believing. It's easy for them to believe in love and goodness,
and God." Doubting Thomas is the role model for others of
us. However, if you are fortunate enough to have faith
genes, so that believing in God comes naturally, you're way
ahead of the more suspicious and cynical.

Werner Von Braun, a father of our space age, said this in
describing science in the twentieth century: "At the end of
the nineteenth century, science had a mind-set about creation, one that came out of the medieval church theology.
God was seen as the Creator who wound up the universe
like a clock and set it off and went on His way. Today science believes that creation is like a divine thought, a great
idea." Perhaps we've come to a time when it's easier for
those faith-genes people to be scientists.

The difficulty of believing the Easter story really begins
much earlier on with the proposition that God, after creat-
ing the heavens and the earth, stepped down into His creation. That idea seems almost ridiculous. Can you imagine
the head of some big industry stepping down from his ex-
alted position to go back on the assembly line, putting rivets
in autos or airplanes? Of course not. Or, can you imagine
Mr. Reagan returning from our nation's capital after his
term of office and running for city council in Santa Barbara?
Absurd.

Even the most humble and dedicated among us find that
sort of move difficult if not impossible. For many of us,

Henri Nouwen has been a contemporary hero. This humble, contemplative Roman Catholic priest and Harvard faculty member has written books that have blessed us all. Nouwen cares about the poor, as you and I must, if we're Jesus people. In 1982 he went to live for a year in a rural Peruvian village. He boarded with a local family caught in desperate poverty. He wrote friends about how difficult it was.

"Can we truly live with the poor? . . . I have been here only one week and thus am unable to have an opinion, but I know one thing: right now I would be physically, mentally and spiritually unable to survive without the opportunity to break away from it all once in a while. All the functions of life, which previously hardly requested attention, are complicated and time-consuming operations here: washing, cooking, writing, cleaning and so on. The winds cover everything with thick layers of dust; water has to be hauled up in buckets from below and boiled to be drinkable; there is seldom a moment of privacy with kids walking in and out all the time; and the thousands of loud sounds make silence a far away dream. . . . I love living here, but I am also glad that I can escape it for two hours a day and for one day a week . . ." (*National Catholic Reporter*, September 17, 1982).

Some years back, when Gustav was king of Sweden, he and the archbishop of the state church were good friends. One day the archbishop came to the king with a request, "Your majesty, there's a vacancy in a tiny church in a little fishing village on a small island in the Baltic Sea. We've been together for a long time, your majesty, but with your permission, I would like to spend my declining years as the pastor of that church."

"Well, old friend, I know that village well. I remember that little church. As a matter of fact, I just learned of the death of the postmaster in that town. I would like nothing better than to cease being king, and spend my declining years as the postmaster in that remote spot with you as my pastor. Unfortunately, you and I are both going to remain right where we are."

That kind of "stepping down" was not a realistic goal for either of those men. But let's consider the incarnation from another perspective. Our oldest son was living in Texas and employed as a journalist when, on a visit to Washington, D.C., he and a friend found a stray puppy wandering on the street. In a fit of compassion, Peter picked him up, bought a portable kennel and flew him back to Texas. Jeff, the stray dog, was his beloved companion until, as the result of a recent accident, his behavior became peculiar—almost deranged. The veterinarian, puzzled by Jeff's problems, suggested he see a dog neurologist. Peter was incredulous. "Did you ever hear of something like that?" he asked us. "Next, I'll be taking him to a dog orthodontist to correct his bite."

The veterinary neurologist diagnosed Jeff's problems as brain damage. Only surgery would save him. It was at this point that Peter suspected the veterinarian had X-ray vision and could look right into both his heart and wallet.

"How much would the operation cost?"

"Two hundred and fifty dollars."

Peter explained, "If he had said three hundred dollars, I would have said, 'Put him to sleep.' He seemed to know that two hundred and fifty dollars was my breaking point. In spite of my guilt about spending such a sum on this mutt, I agreed."

Now, let me ask you dog and cat lovers how much your pet is worth to you. How much would you pay to save him, her, or it? Take this thesis a little further—would you give up your humanity and become a dog to redeem your dog or cat? Of course not. Would you give up the privilege of being a human being with a soul, with a knowledge of God, with your capacity for communication and relationship and creation, and become a dog yourself in order to redeem him? Nobody loves an animal that much. But this is the improbable doctrine we Christians are asked to believe about our Creator. He stepped down and left His creation, His heaven, and became one of us.

We read in the second chapter of Paul's letter to the Philippians, "Have this mind among yourselves, which you have in Christ Jesus, who, though he was in the form of God, did not count equality with God a thing to be grasped, but emptied himself, taking the form of a servant, being born in the likeness of men" (2:5–7 RSV). And John, the beloved apostle, writes in his first chapter: "In the beginning was the Word, and the Word was with God, and the Word was God. He was in the beginning with God; all things were made through him, and without him was not anything made that was made. . . . And the Word became flesh and dwelt among us, full of grace and truth . . ." (1:1–3, 14 RSV).

The Bible doesn't give us the option of believing that God picked out a human being (Jesus) and elevated Him. The shocking fact of the incarnation is that God Himself left His heaven, His privileged domain, and came to live among us. That idea is only the first obstacle to a belief in the Resurrection—that the final resting place of God is not His heaven but, as we read in Revelation, God intends to make His home with us.

As if that were not perplexing enough, there is a second hurdle. Humanly speaking, you and I know that the final resting place for all of us is death and the grave. In spite of all of the stories and legends about vampires and ghouls, about zombies and ghosts, about reincarnation and the walking dead, we know of no one who has ever returned from the grave. The dead are dead. Period. Period. Yet,

central to our faith, is the belief in the Resurrection of the
One who left heaven and lived among us and was totally
man as well as totally God. That belief separates Christianity from every other religion. Think about it. Buddha is
dead. Mohammed is dead. Confucius is dead. Zoroaster is
dead. Gandhi is dead. Marx is dead. Only the Christian
faith claims not only that God became one of us, but that He
died totally and was raised from the dead.

Talleyrand, the famous French statesman, was asked by a
contemporary how he might go about starting a new religion—something more sophisticated than Christianity for
an enlightened France. Talleyrand had this advice, "If you
could manage to be crucified, then entombed for three days,
and ultimately raised from the dead, you might have some
success."

In a recent letter, a friend of mine related a moving story
about the teacher of a third-grade Sunday-school class, a
gifted man and dedicated teacher. In his class of ten young-
sters was a child named Phillip, who suffered from Down's
Syndrome. Children, like their elders, are not always kind to
each other. According to the teacher, the kids were not
overtly mean to Phillip, but neither were they inclusive, and
Phillip didn't seem to fit in.

Last Easter, this teacher had a brilliant idea for presenting
the Easter message. He brought in ten plastic eggs, the kind
that a certain brand of panty hose comes in and gave one to
each of his students with instructions to go outside and find
something that represented new life. The kids were thrilled.
Armed with their eggs, they scrambled all over the church-
yard and the immediate neighborhood.

Back in class, the eggs were opened one by one. The first
contained a butterfly wing—a fitting symbol of the Resurrection and new life. Another one held a bud. Still another had
a flower. One was opened to reveal a stone. The kids' re-

sponse was predictable. "What a dumb thing! Who put that stone in there?" "I did," confessed a little girl belligerently. "I knew you'd all put in buds and flowers and butterfly wings. I wanted to put in something different, because that's what new life means to me." Now there's a budding theologian. When the next egg was opened, it was totally empty. The kids hooted. "Now, that's really dumb! Who did that? Somebody didn't understand the assignment." With that, Phillip pulled on the teacher's coat. "That's my egg," he explained. "It's empty because the tomb is empty. That's what Easter is all about. The tomb is empty."

From that day on, according to the teacher, Phillip was part of the class. The one who brought that profound message to them was totally included. Unfortunately, just three months later little Phillip contracted a disease, one which any child with a normal immune system could have thrown off easily. Phillip, already sickly and frail, died. His third-grade Sunday-school teacher and all nine students went to the funeral. One by one, each child walked to the front of the church to place an item on the coffin—an empty egg. Phillip had taught them all the message of the Resurrection.

But, as we said, the final resting place for the dead, apart from Jesus Christ, is the grave. In Him we are promised resurrection and new life. Where, then, is the final resting place of the Risen Christ? In his letter to the Colossians, Paul writes, ". . . I became a minister according to the divine office which was given to me for you, to make the word of God fully known, the mystery hidden for ages and generations but now made manifest to his saints. To them God chose to make known how great among the Gentiles are the riches of the glory of this mystery, which is *Christ in you,* the hope of glory" (1:25–27 RSV, italics added).

If you and I believe only in the incredible fact of the incarnation, and the astounding truth of the Resurrection, it is of no benefit to us. The third and final resting place of the risen Christ must be in you and me. The Risen One enters into our lives if we are willing to receive Him, and when that happens, according to Paul, we become the hope of glory, the hope of the world.

Pinchas Lapide, a Jewish rabbi, has written a book entitled *The Resurrection of Jesus: A Jewish Perspective.* In it, he insists there is no way that the early church could have begun and spread with such vitality had there not been a Resurrection of Jesus from the dead. This rabbi believes totally in the Resurrection story but, he says, "He was not the Messiah." Belief in the Resurrection did not make the rabbi a Christian. Accepting the Resurrection story is not enough. You and I have got to say, "Lord, come into my life, my heart, and make Your risen home in me."

The Book of Acts tells us that one of the early Christians, Barnabas, traveled to Antioch to check out this new church on behalf of the mother church at Jerusalem. He reported back that he saw "the grace of God" in this new congregation. What did he see? I think he saw people just like us— old, young, black, white, rich, poor—believers in whom Christ lived.

What are some of the signs that He is alive in you, alive in me? I think one of the most important ones is that we are aiming at eternal goals, rather than temporal ones of success, money, fame, or whatever. If you're still fairly young, what is it that you want to do and be for the next forty or fifty years? When I was in high school, the country was still gripped by the Depression. Security and success seemed supremely important. The goal was to make an adequate living in a secure and steady job, or in some respectable profession. In the sixties and seventies, we experienced a large-scale rejection of those meat-and-potato values. The golden life was self-fulfillment. Many dropped out and started a counterculture. But forty or fifty years of pursuing a counterculture can be ultimately just as unrewarding.

A recent story in *The New Yorker* by Frank Gannon suggests that the eighties have produced their own unique set of values. "Once upon a time, and a very good time it was, there was a little boy named George who wanted to learn how to read and speak three languages before he was five and learn how to play the piano and the violin and tennis. And he also wanted to become literate at the computer and learn how to eat a lot of roughage and exercise sensibly and experience excellence."

The world's goals, even the good ones, are transitory. If you believe that Christ lives in you, then your primary goal is to be a witness to the world that God is, that He loves us, that in Jesus He came to live among us, that He died, rose again, and lives in you and me. Our goal is to be a part of a network of people who are committed to being God's underground for changing the way the world lives.

Paul Little, a well-known Christian leader, recently deceased, told about his conversion in this way. He was about ten or twelve when his church sponsored a mission to children. "The missioner lined up a whole bunch of bells on a table with this explanation, 'Now all of these bells have a clapper except one. The bells all look alike and unless you ring each one, you cannot tell which one lacks a clapper. The Christian life is like that. If the Lord lives in you, you have a clapper.'" Young Paul was stabbed. "I knew I didn't have a clapper," he said, "and I gave my life to the Lord that very Sunday."

One evidence that Christ lives in us, I'm convinced, is that we have resources for every situation. We are not afraid to wade in over our heads. We are not afraid that our resources, practical or spiritual, will run out. A friend who is an Episcopal priest tells about the major turning point in his life. He and his wife were driving home from his ordination service when they came upon the scene of a major traffic accident. They pulled over and climbed out of the car to see if they could help. A fourteen-month-old baby riding in one of the cars had been critically injured.

Seeing my friend in his priestly garb, the baby's father rushed over carrying his little girl. "Would you pray for my child, Father?" My friend was at a loss. "You see," he said, "I had never in my life prayed a prayer that I hadn't read in a prayer book." That incident changed his life. "I went home and prayed, 'Lord, when and if that ever happens again I've got to have resources. I want to be somebody in whom You live.'" If Christ lives in us, we have no fear of the future. We can launch out, certain that we have all the resources we need.

The road to the tomb was, in the final analysis, a joyful road for the women who traveled it. Christ was not in the sepulchre. He had come instead to rest in their hearts and in the hearts of all those who believe in Him.

CHRISTIAN HERALD ASSOCIATION AND ITS MINISTRIES

CHRISTIAN HERALD ASSOCIATION, founded in 1878, publishes The Christian Herald Magazine, one of the leading interdenominational religious monthlies in America. Through its wide circulation, it brings inspiring articles and the latest news of religious developments to many families. From the magazine's pages came the initiative for CHRISTIAN HERALD CHILDREN and THE BOWERY MISSION, two individually supported not-for-profit corporations.

CHRISTIAN HERALD CHILDREN, established in 1894, is the name for a unique and dynamic ministry to disadvantaged children, offering hope and opportunities which would not otherwise be available for reasons of poverty and neglect. The goal is to develop each child's potential and to demonstrate Christian compassion and understanding to children in need.

Mont Lawn is a permanent camp located in Bushkill, Pennsylvania. It is the focal point of a ministry which provides a healthful "vacation with a purpose" to children who without it would be confined to the streets of the city. Up to 1000 children between the age of 7 and 11 come to Mont Lawn each year.

Christian Herald Children maintains year-round contact with children by means of a *City Youth Ministry.* Central to its philosophy is the belief that only through sustained relationships and demonstrated concern can individual lives be truly enriched. Special emphasis is on individual guidance, spiritual and family counseling and tutoring. This follow-up ministry to inner-city children culminates for many in financial assistance toward higher education and career counseling.

THE BOWERY MISSION, located at 227 Bowery, New York City, has since 1879 been reaching out to the lost men on the Bowery, offering them what could be their last chance to rebuild their lives. Every man is fed, clothed and ministered to. Countless numbers have entered the 90-day residential rehabilitation program at the Bowery Mission. A concentrated ministry of counseling, medical care, nutrition therapy, Bible study and Gospel services awakens a man to spiritual renewal within himself.

These ministries are supported solely by the voluntary contributions of individuals and by legacies and bequests. Contributions are tax deductible. Checks should be made out either to CHRISTIAN HERALD CHILDREN or to THE BOWERY MISSION.

Administrative Office: 40 Overlook Drive, Chappaqua, New York 10514
Telephone: (914) 769-9000